I0644907

The Experience of Truth

SUNY series in Contemporary Italian Philosophy

Silvia Benso and Brian Schroeder, editors

The Experience of Truth

Gaetano Chiurazzi

Translated by Robert T. Valgenti

SUNY PRESS

Published by State University of New York Press, Albany

Printed in the United States of America

For information, contact State University of New York Press, Albany, NY
www.sunypress.edu

Production, Jenn Bennett
Marketing, Michael Campochiaro

Library of Congress Cataloging-in-Publication Data

Names: Chiurazzi, Gaetano, author.
Title: The experience of truth / Gaetano Chiurazzi ; English translation by Robert T. Valgenti.
Other titles: L'esperienza della verità. Italian
Description: Albany, NY : State University of New York, 2017. | Series: SUNY series in contemporary Italian philosophy | Includes bibliographical references and index.
Identifiers: LCCN 2016047189 (print) | LCCN 2017039126 (ebook) | ISBN 9781438466460 (e-book) | ISBN 9781438466453 (hardcover : alk. paper) | ISBN 9781438466446 (paperback : alk. paper)
Subjects: LCSH: Truth.
Classification: LCC BD171 (ebook) | LCC BD171 .C5413 2017 (print) | DDC 121—dc23
LC record available at https://lccn.loc.gov/2016047189

10 9 8 7 6 5 4 3 2 1

Contents

Introduction

Today one can say of truth what Kant wrote about metaphysics in 1787, namely, that "the changed fashion of the time brings her only scorn; a matron outcast and forsaken, she mourns like Hecuba."[1] And the brief yet effective chronicle of the destiny of metaphysics that Kant traces in the lines immediately following this passage could also be adapted nicely to the destiny of truth:

> Her government, under the administration of the *dogmatists*, was at first *despotic*. But inasmuch as the legislation still bore traces of the ancient barbarism, her empire gradually through intestine wars gave way to complete anarchy; and the *sceptics*, a species of nomads, despising all settled modes of life, broke up from time to time all civil society.[2]

The contemporary debate over truth seems to be caught in a similar situation: between the defense of the metaphysical meaning of truth and its complete negation, between dogmatism and skepticism, or even between absolutism and relativism.[3] However, as Kant attempted in his critique, one ought to ask if the negation of metaphysical knowledge is in fact the negation of all knowledge tout court, or if instead this brings about the valorization of a more "terrestrial," *physical*, form of knowledge that, as Kant would say, is limited to the field of possible experience. The expression "experience of truth" is assumed in this book to have a similar intent, and above all to mark a problematic question: whether it makes any sense to speak of truth as something potentially extraneous to our experience *in general*, or whether it is not instead something intrinsic and constitutive of our experience, real or possible.

In fact it is the return to experience that allows Kant to separate himself both from dogmatic rationalism and also skeptical empiricism, and to resolve, on these grounds, the conflict of reason. The goal of this book is to adopt a strategy similar to the one Kant uses in relation to metaphysics: bringing the problem of truth back to experience, intended not solely in epistemological terms but as the background that constitutes—and results from—every one of our relations with the world. This occurs in the way that Hegel, after Kant, utilized the term: "experience" is for Hegel a formative journey, which implicates not only our relation to the natural world, to objects, but also our relation to the human world, to others and to those "spiritual objects" that are cultural formations.

In my view, the hermeneutic treatment of truth has to be set against such a background. "The experience of truth" is in fact a recurring expression in philosophical hermeneutics: Heidegger refers to the "primordial" experience of truth that the Greeks had when he seeks to illustrate the significance of the word *alétheia*; Gadamer refers to the concrete experience of historical life in his attempt to rehabilitate an extra-methodical dimension of truth that supports the claim to truth of the human sciences.[4] A hermeneutic conception of the experience of truth first of all requires a clarification of the hermeneutic conception of experience, such as the one Gadamer sets forth in the second part of *Truth and Method*. This makes it possible to avoid the risk of intuitionism,[5] namely, to avoid considering the hermeneutic notion of truth as *alétheia* or disclosedness as another formulation of the phenomenological concept of "evidence." For Husserl, evidence is not Cartesian certitude, the imposition upon consciousness of an absolutely true content, but is the pure givenness—the "in the flesh"—of something to consciousness:

> To speak of self-evidence, of self-evident givenness, then, here signifies nothing other than *self-givenness*, the way in which an object in its givenness can be characterized relative to consciousness as "itself there," "there in the flesh," in contrast to its mere presentification [*Vergegenwärtigung*], the empty, merely indicative idea of it.[6]

In comparison to this objectivistic conception of evidence as the apprehension of something simple[7] given to consciousness, in Heidegger evidence is thought rather as a "coming foremost into view." It is defined in relation to a background, as occurs in a game between two elements or between two levels. Now, if there is a difference that radically distinguishes intuition from understanding, it is precisely the fact that the former concerns simple objects and the latter concerns relations,[8] namely, *senses*, understood as forms or modes of relating to something rather than as objects to which a noun refers. In experience, understood in this way and thus in hermeneutical terms as a phenomenon of understanding, we are no longer dealing with objects, but above all with senses, relations, which in turn are only defined on the basis of a point of coordination, namely, the origin-point that for Heidegger is Dasein.

The way that Heidegger develops his "existential analytic" not only recalls a similar chapter in Kant's *Critique of Pure Reason* entitled "The Analytic of Concepts"; I believe it also recalls certain assumptions of the modern scientific revolution that derive from Descartes. Analytic geometry has shown that it is possible to describe the world not by describing *objects*, but *relations*: in order to do this, it is no longer necessary to make reference to some essences, but rather it is necessary to single out an Archimedean point, an origin-point, from which such relations can be established. The deictic definition of Dasein that Heidegger gives in *Being and Time* is, in my view, nothing other than the transposition onto a semantic plane of the revolution brought about by Descartes's analytic geometry in the physical field: the describability of the world (understood as a web of senses) is grounded in the same principle that allows the describability of physical space—the definition of an origin-point. In my view, one can thus with good reason speak of a "Cartesian aspect" in Heidegger, which does not consist in the resumption of the metaphysics of the *cogito*, as happens with Husserl, even if it lacks its apodictic moment, but in the resumption of the methodological formulation of analytic geometry: the invention of a system of coordinates that for Heidegger have their zero point in Dasein, namely, in that "absolute deixis" that is the *Sum*. According to Heidegger, no description of the world can leave out the deictic reference to this *Sum*. The result of this "semantic schema" is that there is no longer sense[9] (and therefore, a fortiori, truth) without Dasein, which involves neither a negation nor a subjectification of truth, but the elaboration of a concept of truth *formally* more complex than the traditional version,[10] more complex than the representational notion of truth, understood thus as the simple correspondence to sensorial data or a state of affairs. Only in this way can the full semantic content of truth finally be appreciated.

What in fact do we mean when we say that something "is true"? A hermeneutic approach to the problem of truth must begin with this question, which is not the question "what is" truth, but rather a question about its significance in our experience. Posing the question in these terms demonstrates the insufficiency, from a formal point of view, of the idea that truth—independent of any experience of things and "whoever" enters into a relation with them—is a sort of property of the state of affairs. And, from a semantic point of view, it leads to the refutation of the thesis of equivalence, which turns truth into something merely redundant, by instead defending its ability to "make sense." When we say that something "is true" we are not only saying something about the state of affairs, but also about ourselves: in particular, we affirm that in our experience something has changed, has come "to the fore," and we thus indicate a dispositional transformation in our relation with the world. Truth is a *mode* of experience, the index of its reorientation, and thus of a change in sense. Only by bringing truth back to the realm of experience—and thus, only if one arrives at a different understanding of its formal structure—can its semantic content be rehabilitated. Far from being a sign of an atemporal reality, or of the abyss between an eternal reality and our experience, truth is on the contrary exactly what makes reality "in itself" a reality "for us": what connects us to reality by making it precisely into *our* world, rather than some other, independent world.

Chapter 1 (Before Judgment) is dedicated to the Heideggerian analysis of the concept of truth, in order to show that the polemic against the traditional conception of truth as correspondence does not imply its negation but affirms only its derivative and secondary character: what is in fact more originary is the ontological determination of truth as *alétheia*. This analysis is forwarded by discussing the Aristotelian definition of apophantic discourse presented in *De interpretatione*, which suggests a very peculiar understanding of the verb *hypárchein*, "to inhere" (according to Boethius's translation), but also of the verb "to exist" (as is found above all beginning from the Hellenistic period).

Chapter 2 (*Verbum Consignificat Tempus*) follows the discussion taken up in chapter 1 by moving on to an analysis of the meaning of the copula in Aristotle, and in particular of its *consignificatio temporis*: a sense that clearly constitutes a thread that leads to the Kantian thematization of time as the form of every relationship to objects (and thus as the essential form of every experiential truth), and from here to the Heideggerian understanding of Being as time. This chapter begins with a comparison between linguistic locutions without the copula (the nominal sentence) and those with the copula, by discussing their diverse roles in the expression of truth in order to show, on the one hand, the specificity of the sentence with the copula, and on the other hand, its generality, since the lack of the copula is in the nominal sentence only apparent. In every expression of truth, time is also understood-with [*con-compreso*], not as the time of the event being expressed, but as the time of the utterance. That brings about a structural reconfiguration of the concept of truth, in which space-time relations and, in the end, the very subject of the proposition are also taken into account.

Chapter 3 (The Experience of Truth as the Experience of Time) is dedicated to showing how the Heideggerian notion of *alétheia* returns to an experiential dimension. *Alétheia* does not allude, as one might be led to believe, to the idea that some concealed thing exists alongside some disclosed thing, namely that truth has a hidden basis behind what is shown; rather, *alétheia* points to the experience of the existing thing and its possible nonbeing: it is the very experience of time and of contingency. The ontology presupposed by philosophical hermeneutics is in fact the ontology of history and of ethics as it has been articulated since Aristotle: the ontology of not only what could be different from how it now is, but also of what could not even be.

In Chapter 4 (Truth and Transformation) a conception of truth as "transformational operator" is proposed, according to which the predicate "true" does not indicate the simple subsistence of the state of affairs but is rather the sign of a transformation that has occurred within our experience. This thesis is confirmed through a critical encounter with pragmatism, and with Richard Rorty's pragmatic-nihilistic declinations of hermeneutics. Against the basically verificationist conception of pragmatism, what is instead proposed is a conception of truth in falsificationist terms, founded on the Gadamerian concept of experience set forth in *Truth and Method*, in which the role of the negative is fundamental, as it was in the corresponding Hegelian concept. The transformational significance of truth is already present in Plato's allegory of the cave, in which the experience of truth is at the same time an experience of emancipation and of freedom.

Chapter 5 (More Than the Real) is concerned with the concept of truth that Gadamer elaborates in *Truth and Method*, in order to defend the extra-methodological nature of the experience of truth proper to the human sciences. This is understood, on the one hand, upon the ontological background developed in chapter 3 (the ontology of the contingent), and on the other hand, through the concepts of play, representation, and images, as indicators of a "surplus," of an increase in being with respect to simple reality. Truth is thus the presentation of reality in a different modality, in an intensively enriched dimension. This increase constitutes the more properly formative aspect of truth, the idea that through the consciousness of the true being, a different articulation of the real stands forth—what Gadamer called "transformation into form."

Chapter 6 (The Sense of Truth) is dedicated to a critical analysis of the Nietzschean concept of truth, beginning from the problematization of its presumed nihilistic character (truth as the expression of metaphysics). There the question is raised whether one can also affirm that truth's sense depends, as with every other concept, on the force which appropriates it. This could suggest that there is (or there can be) a non-nihilistic sense of truth, one that is demonstrated through a commentary on some of the aphorisms in *Daybreak*.

Chapter 7 (A Non-alienated Conception of Truth) discusses the alternative to the hermeneutic conception of truth represented by Hilary Putnam's definition of metaphysical realism. The way that truth is conceptualized in metaphysical realism (however the same could be said, mutatis mutandis, of empiricism, subjectivism, and idealism) necessarily cuts away "pieces" of our world (and even ourselves) by rendering an alienated image of truth. A non-alienated conception of truth, such as the one proposed by philosophical hermeneutics, integrates such elements into what is here called "experience," and what Heidegger calls "being-in-the-world": this entails a reevaluation of the semans tic content of the predicate "true" (against the correspondence theory) and also the defense of its nonrepresentational character. The eccentricity of truth with respect to method is in the end understood, on the basis of a discussion about the relation between truth and power in Michel Foucault, as the sign of its power to liberate from oppression, of its concrete capacity to produce emancipation and reverse alienation.

Some of the following chapters resume arguments and theses already presented in works published in recent years in various journals and books. Even if published separately, these essays suggest a precise comprehensive design that is on this occasion taken up again and in some instances developed rather deeply.

Chapter 1 resumes an essay published in German with the title "Die Antezedens der Wahrheit. Heidegger und die Aristotelische Definition der apoe phantischen Rede" in *Existentia: International Journal of Philosophy* 17 (2007): 1–17.

Chapter 2 was published with the title "Verbum consignificat tempus: Sulla dimensione verbale della verità" in *Filosofia e Espiritualidade: O contributo da Idade Média (Philosophy and Spirituality in the Middle Ages), Revista Portuguesa de Filosofia*, 64, no. 1 (2008): 577–594, edited by João J. Vila-Chã. I am grateful to the editor, who has granted permission for its republication.

Chapter 3 has not been published previously.

Chapter 4 was published with the title "Per una concezione trasformazionale della verità: ermeneutica e pragmatismo" in *Pensare L'attualità, cambiare il mondo. Confronto con Gianni Vattimo,* edited by G. Chiurazzi (Milano: Bruno Mondadori, 2008), 97–111.

Chapter 5 is based on a presentation with the title "Truth is More Than Reality," given at the International Conference "Wozu Hermeneutik? 50 Years since *Truth and Method*" at the Fifth Annual Meeting of the North American Society for Philosophical Hermeneutics, Seattle, September 16–18, 2010. That paper was published in *Research in Phenomenology* 41, no. 1 (Leiden: Koninklijke Brill NV 2011), 60–71.

Chapter 6 was published with the title "Il senso della verità: critica e nichilismo" in *Nietzsche y la hermenéutica* 2, edited by F. Arenas-Dolz, L. Giancristofaro, and P. Stellino (Valencia: Guada Impresora, 2007), 831–839. Thanks to Prof. Francisco Arenas-Dolz of the University of Valencia for granting permission to republish the essay.

Chapter 7 has not been published previously.

Chapter 1

Before Judgment

Judgment and Truth

A discussion of the problem of truth cannot avoid beginning with the problem of its relation to judgment, traditionally considered the very locus of truth. The question is posed by Heidegger in §44 of *Being and Time*. In this section, Heidegger attempts to "destruct" the traditional definition of truth, an operation that is one of the fundamental stages of the complex strategy that guides the research on the meaning of being in general, the aim of which, as explained in §6, is to loosen a consolidated tradition, "until we arrive at those primordial experiences in which we achieved our first ways of determining the nature of being—the ways which have guided us ever since."[1] In the case of truth, Heidegger's argument moves first from its traditional definition as *adequatio intellectus et rei,* which is articulated in three theses:

> (1) that the "locus" of truth is assertion (judgment); (2) that the essence of truth lies in the "agreement" of the judgment with its object; (3) that Aristotle, the father of logic, not only has assigned truth to the judgment as its primordial locus but has set going the definition of "truth" as "agreement."[2]

The destruction of these theses is a complex procedure in which the destructuring return converges with the recovery of the authentic Aristotelian understanding of truth. The result of this return leads to a real overturning, an inversion of the first of the three theses, which Heidegger tries to confirm in Aristotle himself: judgment is not the locus of truth, but rather truth is the locus of judgment. For Heidegger, this antepredicative truth coincides with being-in-the-world, namely, with the disclosedness of Dasein.

Here we should not be interested in the consequences of this Heideggerian argument as regards the conception of truth as correspondence, but rather with its premises, by trying at the same time to follow the thread of its legitimacy that Heidegger claims to have rediscovered in Aristotle. It cannot be denied that at first glance the claim "the judgment is in truth" appears to be contrary to the Aristotelian text, and in particular to the definition of apophantic discourse in *De Interpretatione* 4,17a 1–3, to which most traditional interpretations typically refer. In this passage from *De Interpretatione* Aristotle in fact claims: "Every sentence has meaning (not as a tool but, as we said, by convention), but not every sentence is a proposition—only those in which there is truth or falsity (*en ô tò aletheúein è pseùdesthai hypárchei*)." To the letter, so it seems, Aristotle says precisely that the true and the false are in discourse. Heidegger nevertheless insists that the discourse is in truth, and thus that discourse *presupposes aletheúein* and *pseúdesthai*, namely, as it translates when respecting the verbal character of these expressions, that discourse presupposes disclosure and concealment as attitudes of Dasein. Truth is thus the *ontological* condition of judgment.

How is such a claim possible? Does it not risk being philologically incorrect, or even completely arbitrary? The thesis I would like to put forward is that Heidegger's claim has its own legitimacy, and I will try to show (1) its correspondence to the authentic meaning of Aristotle's claim; and (2) the reason for this inverse formulation. Rather than follow the phenomenological analyses through which Heidegger tries to justify his interpretation,[3] I will instead attempt to justify it based on Aristotle's definition of apophantic discourse, by trying to understand the meaning of the expression *en ô tò aletheúein è pseùdesthai hypárchei,* and in particular, the meaning of the construction *en ô hypárchei*, which articulates the relation between truth and judgment.

Hypárchein en tiní: Ontological Antecedence

The expression *hypárchein en tiní* appears in many places in Aristotle's works. One of the more important instances is in the *Categories*, precisely where he addresses the distinction between primary and secondary substances. Here Aristotle writes:

> The species in which the things primarily called substances are (*en oîs eídesin hypárchousin*), are called *secondary substances*, as also are the genera

> of these species. For example, the individual man belongs (*hypárchei*) in a species, man, and animal is a genus of the species; so these—both man and animal—are called secondary substances.[4]

The translations found in the principal European languages confirm the idea that the construction *hypárchein en tiní* alludes to "being contained in something."[5] What this might mean is not at all clear. We can above all take note that Aristotle distinguishes here two forms of inclusion:

1. inclusion in a subject (*eînai en tiní*);
2. inclusion in a second substance or predicate (*hypárchein en tiní*).

They are incompatible, since in the first case the predicates are in their subjects, while in the second case the subject (primary substance, which on the other hand cannot be other than the subject) exists in its substantial predicates (secondary substances). The primary substances therefore exist in their secondary substances, but, as subjects, include their accidents.

The primary substances are thus "in" the secondary substances, but not as these latter are in subjects: in fact, Aristotle writes, "It is a characteristic common to every substance not to be in a subject (*mè en hypokeiménō eînai*)."[6] And a bit later he reaffirms:

> We need not be disturbed by any fear that we may be forced to say that the parts of a substance, being in a subject (the whole substance), are not substances. For when we speak of things *in a subject* (*hōs en hypokeiménois ónta*) we did not mean things *existing* [my italics] in something as *parts* (*tà hōs mérē hypárchonta én tini*).[7]

There are therefore two ways of "being in," distinct through a terminological differentiation: *eînai* is used for the accidental relation, *hypárchein* for the substantial relation. The meaning of inclusion is also different: the accidental predicates *are* in their subjects, while the primary substance (that can only be subject) *exists* (as the Italian translation conveniently states) in its substantial predicates (the secondary substances). Why didn't Aristotle use the verb *eînai* for this second way of "being included"? Probably because in this case the relation defined as *hypárchein en tiní* would have been reduced to a predicative relation, which Aristotle clearly wanted to avoid.

The difference between *eînai* and *hypárchein* is fundamental and therefore distinguishing: C. H. Kahn observes that in contrast to *eînai*, *hypárchein* carries a temporal connotation of antecedence, the sense of a "being before," as with a principle (although not in the causal sense).[8] *Hypárchonta* are the circumstances, the conditions, the resources or means that they have at their disposal because something happens; it its impersonal use, *hypárchei* means "is given, the fact is." Originarily, *hypárchein* in fact signifies "to begin" or "to take initiative" or "to make the first attempt" in completing something. This connotation is particularly clear in its absolute use:

> In this absolute use *hypárchō* means not "to make a beginning" (in doing something) but "to *be* a beginning," "to be on hand (from the beginning, at the start)." In this use *hypárchō* is practically a synonym for *páreimi* "to be present with," "to be available for." In the most natural and typical cases, the temporal sense of "previously," or "already, at the start" is clearly implied.[9]

As a variant of *árchein* ("to command, to order, to begin") with the prefix *hypó* ("under") added, *hypárchein* thus alludes to an implicit or underlying principality that introduces a relation of dependence or of subordination.

"Being present from the beginning" is thus not so much a relation of spatial inclusion, but a relation of condition/conditioned: whatever *hypárchei* (is given) must be there because something happens, but that does not mean that what happens follows due to the simple fact that there is that something. It therefore constitutes a *necessary* but not *sufficient* condition. By speaking of primary substances, Aristotle in fact says that without them neither the secondary substances nor any other thing would exist.[10] The primary substances "are" *already* in the secondary substances in the sense that *they precede them from an ontological point of view*. The substantial predicates (but the discourse could easily be generalized to every type of predicate) do not exist in themselves, but exist only because the primary substances *already* exist (this is the core of Aristotle's polemic against the separate existence of the ideas maintained by Plato).

Hypárchein tiní: The Essential Antecedence

Aristotle, however, uses the verb *hypárchein* also to express another type of relation: this deals with the expression found above all in the *Prior and*

Posterior Analytics, "*tò* B *tô* A *hypárchei*," normally translated as "B (namely, the predicate) belongs to A." Such a form is thus considered equivalent to the copulative form "A is B,"[11] where it expresses a necessary connection, such that it is convertible with it, even though the opposite is not possible:

> The conversion of an appropriate name which is derived from an accident is an extremely precarious thing; for in the case of accidents and in no other it is possible for something to be true in a certain respect and not universally. Names derived from definition and property and genus are bound to be convertible; e.g. if being a two-footed terrestrial animal belongs to something (*hypárchei tini*), then it will be true by conversion to say that it is a two-footed terrestrial animal. Likewise, also, if derived from the genus; for if being an animal belongs to something, then it is an animal.[12]

Hypárchein tiní expresses a necessary relation between the subject and predicate, that of subsumption, which excludes identity.[13]

The distinctions that we have up to this point developed can thus be summarized according to the following schema:

1. *eînai en tiní* — to be in a subject (predicative relation of the accidental type)
2. *hypárchein tiní* — to belong to (predicative relation of the substantial type)
3. *hypárchein en tiní* — to exist in something (existential relation)

The primary substance therefore "exists in secondary substances" in the sense that it is its condition of possibility. These secondary substances, conversely, *belong* to the primary substances, in the sense that they are *part* of their essential definition. Therefore, only this is a true predicative relation, as it is impossible for the primary substances to be predicated of anything.

Contemporary logic uses "belonging" to indicate the relation between individual and species, and "inclusion" to indicate the relation between species and genus, according to a relation of increasing extension. These two relations are analytically distinct, respectively, through the functor of belonging "∈" (Peano) and that of inclusion "⊃" (Gergonne). Aristotle has been rebuked for not distinguishing "the relation of inclusion among classes from the relation of the belonging of an individual to a class. It is always a matter of *hypárchein*: in the first case, of the genus to the species, in the second of the species to the individual. He therefore supposed that the relation was the same in both cases. [. . .]"[14] This analysis is not, however, completely true. Aristotle, as we have seen, clearly distinguishes these two relations, not by referring to two distinct lexemes, but to two different syntactical constructions of the same lexeme, or to be precise, of the verb *hypárchein*: by now, one can say that Aristotle uses the expression "belonging to" and "being included" (or better: "being in")—or at least in this way they make for equivalent translations, as one sees from those noted in note 5—in a manner directly opposed to how it is done in set-theory.

The different syntactic construction—prepositional (*en tinì*) or with the simple dative (*tinì*)—ought instead to be understood as the reference to an existential (ontological) dimension or to a predicative (logico-discursive) dimension, to which there correspond two different types of necessity:

a1. *Hypárchein en tiní* expresses the idea that the primary substance (A) is the necessary condition of the existence of the secondary substance (B) which would not exist without it;

a2. *Hypárchein tiní* expresses the idea that the predicates are a necessary condition of the definition of the subject, to which they belong essentially: if there were not these predicates, that subject would not be what it is.

It would thus be a matter of the distinction between an existential relation and a definitional relation, between existence and essence, between *that it is* and *what it is*. In both cases, the meaning of the temporal anteriority of the verb *hypárchein* is preserved: as ontological antecedence or as essential antecedence (according to the Aristotelian definition of essence, which indicates what the subject was *already, tò tí en eînai*). That these relations should not be considered equivalent is shown by the fact that, while *a2* can be immediately converted into the predicative form ($S \supset P$ equals "S is P"), *a1* cannot be: one cannot say that a given secondary substance *is* a certain primary substance, and that affirms precisely the resistance of the relation *hypárchein en tiní* to predication. It expresses instead an *antepredicative* relation, which precedes every predication and makes it possible: without the primary substances there would be no secondary substances, and even more so, no accidents. The translation of *hypárchein* as "to exist"—and of the substantive *hyparxis* as "existence," above all since the Hellenistic period[15]—only confirms this interpretation: primary substance here tends to be confused with the very notion of "existence," as the ontological *prius* of any other predicate. Its characteristic of "category" tends therefore to lessen and instead inclines toward an ontological modality, that of the entity that exists in itself, the *tóde ti*. In short, this could constitute an implicit formulation of the idea, found in Kant, that *existence is not a real predicate*: it is not a predicate that should be part of the essential definition of a subject because, in general, *it is not a predicate at all.*

The *Inesse*: From Boethius to Leibniz

That existence, and as a result truth—whose relation to the discourse is of the same type as that of primary substance with secondary substances—were fallaciously considered as "predicates" is thus an error that also has a linguistic basis. This misunderstanding was probably cemented into place by Boethius, who translated the verb *hypárchein* as *inesse*, "to be contained in." This terminological choice made it so that at a certain point both the form *hypárchein en tiní* and also the form *hypárchein tiní,* were placed in the same conceptual realm, even though Aristotle had kept them far apart. Moreover, the predication defined by Aristotle as "*eînai en tiní*" (it is also a way of "being in," but one that concerns intercategorial or accidental predication) was also added to it. One could compare the Latin translation, already cited in note 5 (the passage from Aristotle in which the relation between primary substance and secondary substances is defined), to the use that Boethius made of the verb *inesse* to indicate the accidental relation. In a passage from his commentary on *De Interpretatione*, Boethius writes:

> Dicit autem esse verbum semper eorum quae de altero praedicantur notam, quod huiusmodi est ac si diceret nihil aliud nisi accidentia verba signifi care. Omne enim verbum aliquod accidens designat. Cum enim dico cursus, ipsum quidem est accidens, sed non ita dicitur ut id alicui inesse vel non inesse dicatur. Si autem dixero currit, tunc ipsum accidens in alicuius actione proponens alicui inesse significo.[16]

The expression "B *inest* A" thus becomes, starting from Boethius, the canonical form for expressing the relation between subject (A) and predicate (B) as the general relation of "inherence." *Inesse* appears as an ambiguous term that, besides reducing the antepredicative relation (*hypárchein en tiní*) to a predicative one, does not in any way allow for distinguishing between the *meaning* and the *mode* of the relation between subject and predicate. Leibniz is connected to this use, who defined the predicative relation in general as *inesse* by understanding it as *the inclusion of the predicate in the subject*, and by justifying his thesis in this way:

> Therefore the predicate or consequent is always in the subject or antecedent, and the nature of truth in general, i.e. the connection between the terms of a proposition, consists in this very thing, as Aristotle has also observed. And indeed, in identities this connection and inclusion of the predicate in the subject is explicit, whereas in all other truths it is implicit and must be shown through the analysis of concepts, on which *a priori* demonstration is founded.[17]

This reference to Aristotle is justly contested by scholars: to understand the relation of *inesse* in the way that Leibniz did in fact brings about a distortion of the Aristotelian distinctions between the relation *hypárchein en tiní* (which we have defined as "ontological"), the relation *hypárchein tiní* (which we have defined as "essential"), and the relation *eînai en tiní* (accidental). *Inesse* in this case indicates the subject-predicate relation, and in a way that the predicates are contained, *implicated*, in the subject, in the form A ⊃ B: for Leibniz, the subject is the antecedent of a relation of implication, of which the predicate is the consequent. The difference from the relation *hypárchein en tiní* described by Aristotle is thus clear: while Aristotle posits the subject as the consequent (or even as the necessary condition) of the predicate, for Leibniz the opposite is the case. To the end of showing it graphically, we can thus write the first in the form (*a*1) "B → A," and the second in the form (*a*2) "A ⊃ B."

1. *a*1 signifies that the consequent is the *ontological* condition of possibility for the antecedent, which would not exist without it. The *modus tollens* of this implication corresponds to the Aristotelian claim according to which, if there were no primary substance, there would be no secondary substances.

2. *a*2, in the opposite manner, expresses the meaning of the relation of Leibnizian inherence: the subject includes all of its predicates, which constitutes its explication. One finds here the logical form of

> "the principle of sufficient reason," which is the logico-metaphysical equivalent of the ontological constitution of the monads: "*The complete or perfect concept of an individual substance contains* (*involvit*) *all of its predicates*, past, present and future,"[18] which are contained in it (*in rei notione continentur*).

As we have seen, while *a*2 can be immediately transformed into a predicative form ("A ⊃ B" is equivalent to "A is B"), for *a*1 this is not possible. This shows the undeniable resistance of the relation *hypárchein en tiní* to the predicative form and expresses the idea that the primary substance cannot ever be the sufficient condition of its predicates, as instead happens in Leibniz with the concept of the monad.

Once the monad is set, so too are all of its predicates. That explains how for Leibniz the relation of inherence, even if only virtual, is in the end resolved into a relation of identity, in an *idem esse*. All truths, Leibniz writes, can be traced back to identical truths, from the most complex to the most basic, and these to the most primary truths, which are nothing but the predications of identity of the type "A = A":

> Now it is evident that every true predication has some basis in the nature of things, and even when a proposition is not identical, that is, when the predicate is not expressly contained in the subject, it is still necessary that it be virtually contained in it, and this is what philosophers call *in-esse*, saying thereby that the predicate is in the subject.[19]

The equivalence between subject and predicate is thus possible only if any condition of asymmetry is eliminated, whether it is logical or, above all, ontological: namely, *temporal*. The truths that do not possess such symmetry are in fact the truths in which the connection between the subject and the predicate varies in time and is not stable—contingent truths.[20] Their reduction to truths of reason thus brings to the fore the cancellation of their temporal character; their apriority is equal to an *absence of time*. The relation of equivalence therefore supposes the coincidence, at least *virtual*, of accidental relation and substantial relation: as has been suggested, this relation is prepared through the very way in which Boethius understood *inesse*.

The equivalence of truths of fact and truths of reason, of the logical order with the ontological order, is nevertheless possible, according to Leibniz, only for a divine intellect, which is the only one capable of capturing the totality of historical predicates and thus their equivalence with the subject about which they are predicated: the nature of an individual substance or of a complete being is such by being sufficient to understand and to deduce from it all of its possible predicates, even those determinations that we can understand only through history and that we thus call "accidentals."[21] In this way, Leibniz achieves the complete reduction of the problem of truth to one of predication. On the contrary, in Aristotle the relation that he calls *hypárchein en tiní* constitutes a relation that is not predicative and not reducible to Leibnizian *inesse*. In fact, it constitutes the point of greatest resistance against making judgment a complete matter of logic, whose inscription onto a theological background (a background of possible *infinity*, unknown to Aristotle), turns the predicative relation into an analytic relation of the inclusion of the predicate in the subject, and in the end a relation of identity—the result of which is one of the most radical outcomes of eighteenth-century rationalism, and whose effects reach all the way to Hegel by equating contingent truths and necessary truths, the accidental relation with the substantial relation, truths of fact with those of reason.

The Presupposition of Truth

At this point let us return to the Aristotelian definition of apophantic discourse: "Every sentence has meaning (not as a tool but, as we said, by convention), but not every sentence is a proposition—only those in which there is truth or falsity (*en ô tò aletheúein è pseùdesthai hypárchei*)."

Commenting on this definition in its Boethian translation (*Enunciativa vero non omnis (oratio), sed in qua verum vel falsum inest*), 22 Heidegger writes:

> The only speech that indicatively shows something, [and thus is a statement,] is speech in which uncovering or covering-over is present. The Greek word that we translate as "is present," is *hypárchein*, "to be there." But in this case it does not have the meaning it often can, namely, "occurring" in the quite broad sense of "there is something," as if Aristotle meant to say: "Only such speech is indicative in which uncovering and covering-over occurs"—as if covering and uncovering could sometimes occur, and sometimes not. Here, instead, *hypárchein* has the weighty sense of the philosophical concept that is used by Aristotle: *hypárchein* means "being there a priori," "underlying something in such a way that

> everything else is sustained by this thing that is there a priori." For that reason Boethius translates the Greek *hypárchein* in an entirely correct way as "in-*esse*," "being-within-[something]," in this case: "belonging to the very essence of speaking."[23]

Heidegger here understands the *inesse* of Boethius in the authentic Aristotelian sense and in particular shows that he clearly understands the significance of the anteriority proper to the verb *hypárchein*: "Aristotle says *en ô . . . hypárchei*, a discourse is propositional through *aletheúein è pseúdesthai* not merely being found in it, but *lying in it as underlying it*, as contributing toward its *ground* and its *essence*."[24] Only in this way, as we have seen, does the connection between *hypárchein* and essence become understandable, which otherwise in Boethius's use of the verb *inesse* would be completely unexplainable. Truth is the "past" of discourse, what precedes it as its necessary condition of possibility: without truth there would be no discourse. In fact, Heidegger writes, if there were also no discourse, it would not be for this reason that truth would not be: "even when nobody *judges*, truth already gets presupposed in so far as Dasein is at all."[25]

Now, the traditional thesis translates the Aristotelian claim into a spatial language that in fact betrays its meaning. Whatever *hypárchei* thus becomes the "content" and therefore something that presupposes its own container, thus completely inverting the relation of temporal anteriority. In accordance with this spatial language, Heidegger then reformulates the relation of anteriority between truth and discourse by saying, not that truth *is in* discourse, but on the contrary, that *discourse is in truth*:

> Not only is it wrong to invoke Aristotle for the thesis that the genuine "locus" of truth lies in the judgment; even in its content this thesis fails to recognize the structure of truth. *On the contrary*, whether as a mode in which uncoveredness is appropriated or as a way of Being-in-the-world, assertion is grounded in Dasein's uncovering, or rather, its *disclosedness*. The most primordial "truth" is the "locus" of assertion; it is the ontological condition for the possibility that assertions can be either true or false—that they may uncover or cover things up.[26]

In the passage from temporal representation to spatial relation, the relation of antecedence becomes a relation of inclusion, while the antepredicative relation becomes a predicative one. But for Heidegger, the fact that Aristotle, in the definition of apophantic discourse, did not use the adjectives *alethés* and *pseudés*, but the verbs *aletheúein* and *pseúdesthai*, signifies that discourse is grounded in a faculty, the possibility of a comportment for Dasein, a disclosing (true) attitude or a concealing (false) one.

> As assertion, the *lógos apophantikós* certainly has the possibility of being true or being false, but this manner of being true, of becoming manifest, is grounded in a manifestness which, because it lies *prior* to *predication* and the assertion, we designate as *pre-predicative manifestness*, or better, as *pre-logical truth*. "Logical" is here taken in a quite rigorous sense, namely having to do with the *lógos apophantikós* in the form we have interpreted it.[27]

It is therefore in order to confirm the authentic content of the Aristotelian thesis—the idea that truth is the *ontological condition* of discourse, what precedes it and grounds it—that Heidegger has inverted the traditional thesis. As the container precedes the content spatially (it is its *foundation*), one will have to say then that truth is the locus of discourse, and not the other way around. The true foundation, therefore, is truth.

The discussion surrounding the meaning of the expression *hypárchein en tiní* thus shows, in conclusion, that truth cannot be understood as a predicate, as predicates—Leibniz says—are what are contained, implicated in a subject. Its "antepredicative" character is what for Heidegger coincides with the very existence of Dasein:

> The truth which has been presupposed, or the "there is" by which its Being is to be defined, has that kind of Being—or meaning of Being—which belongs to Dasein itself. We must "make" the presupposition of truth because it *is* one that has been "made" already with the Being of the "we."[28]

Truth carries with itself the necessity of a presupposition, or even of the facticity of Dasein as "being *already* in": thus, Heidegger specifies, "It is not we who presuppose 'truth'; but it is '*truth*' that makes it at all possible ontologically for us to be able to *be* such that we 'presuppose' anything at all. Truth is what first *makes possible* anything like presupposing."[29] Truth—like existence—in this way expresses a condition of *absolute* antecedence in respect to discourse: its "interiority" to discourse is nothing other than its *anteriority* in respect to discourse.

Chapter 2

Verbum Consignificat Tempus

The Nominal Phrase: The Presence and the Absence of the Copula

There is a time of truth. With this expression we do not want to say that truth is relative to time, but rather that the concept of truth itself carries with it an unavoidably temporal consignification which is presented first of all in the form of antecedence, of the *a priori*. This temporal understanding makes it so that the concepts of truth and of time cannot be considered opposed and mutually exclusive: even the idea of an "eternal" truth supposes, at its core, an understanding of time. In this way, to say that there is a time of truth means placing the problem of the truth of time in the foreground.

In the previous chapter the truth of time, in the Aristotelian definition of apophantic discourse, was shown to be a temporal antecedence of truth in respect to discourse—an antecedence that, as is evident from the meaning of the verb *hypárchein,* tends toward its existential meaning. Just as primary substance (the *tóde ti*, the "this here") precedes the secondary substances, so too do truth, and especially in Heidegger's case, Dasein (to which he attributes the same purely deictic constitution of the primary substances), precede discourse. It is what we have called the "Cartesian aspect" of Heideggerian philosophy: the idea that every relation with entities, every possible description of the world (and thus every judgment and every truth) is possible only by first defining an origin-point, the methodological revolution on the basis of which analytic geometry has been invented. For Heidegger, this fundamental semantic point of coordination—the focal point of the spatiality of Dasein—is represented by the deictic nature of existence.

In this chapter we will try to develop this theme in another direction, by showing how the temporal sense that ties discourse to its truth-bearing preѳ supposition (namely, to Dasein) is implicit in the very structuring of judgment, and in fact is carried by the copula. It is a question that was posed in a very clear manner by Emile Benveniste in an essay published in 1950 and later included in the volume *Problems in General Linguistics* (1966). In this essay Benveniste compares the phrase without a copula, the nominal phrase, to the phrase that contains the copula—two linguistic formulations common in Indo-European languages. Between them there exists a functional difference: while the nominal phrase is used for general, sententious, atemporal, non-modal claims that are thereby reduced to their exclusive semantic content, phrases with the copula are used for the narration of a fact or for the description of a situation, and thus imply a temporal relation with the speaker. Whereas the phrase with the copula is found often in historical writings, for example in Herodotus, the nominal phrase (which one finds in the most dissimilar linguistic families: Semitic, Finno-Ugric, Bantu, Sumerian, Egyptian, Caucasian, Altaic, Dravidian, Indonesian, Siberian, Amerindian, etc.) is typical of sententious and doctrinal texts—it announces a truth that stands outside of time, persons and circumstances and perfectly sticks to sententious and proverbial proclamations to which it otherwise tends to limit itself. This functional difference is present in all of the Indo-European languages: in addition to Greek and Latin, it is also in Sanskrit, where the contrast, Benveniste writes,

> can be illustrated by (1) *tvám váruṇaḥ* "You are Varuṇa," an absolute homology set up between Agni, to whom one addresses oneself, and Varuṇa, with whom he is identified, and (2) the formula *tat tvam asi* "hoc tu es," which shows man his present condition. The nominal phrase in Vedic is the perfect expression of the timeless *definition*. If in Old Iranian, the nominal phrase abounds in the Gāthās, in which there is not a single example of the phrase with *asti*, this hinges upon the nature of the Gāthās: a brusque catechism, a sequence of assertions of truth and rigid definition, an authoritarian reminder of revealed principles. In the epic narrative fragments of the Yašts, in contrast, the verbal phrase with *asti* regains its rights.[1]

The absence of the copula would therefore be the indicator of a truth without time that in its content is reduced to a claim of absolute identity; instead, the presence of the copula temporally contextualizes truth. The phrase with the copula adds something to the simple nominal content—constituted by the mere juxtaposition without any copulative connection—which is not properly nominated, even though it is understood, and in fact, understood together *with* that same content: this "something" is time. And even though it means time in some way, it does not however necessarily mean that what is expressed is something that develops *in* time, a process or an action, almost as if the copula assumes in itself the character of becoming. The temporality signified by the copula consists rather in the placement of the sentence in relation to the speaker, to whose situation it makes reference. The copula expresses time by binding the sentence to the speaker.

This bond is surely different than the one that simply connects the predicate to the subject in a sentence of the form "S is P." Benveniste in fact identifies in this second type of bond the proper function of the verb, by distinguishing the verbal form from the verbal function (although the two could coincide in the same linguistic expression). The verbal function is purely syntactic, distinct in its "cohesive function," through which the elements of a sentence are organized into a complete structure, and its "assertive function," through which the sentence is granted its real status. The first is a grammatical relationship "that unites the members of the sentence"; the second "*adds* implicitly a 'this *is*!' that links the linguistic arrangement to the system of reality."[2]

> Thus the syntactic structure of the finite assertion helps to distinguish two planes: the plan of grammatical cohesion, on which the verb serves as the cohering element, and the plane of the assertion of reality, from which the verb receives its functions as the assertive element. In a finite assertive sentence the verb possesses this double capacity.[3]

"Verb" is not therefore the grammatical element that indicates a process (there are languages that indicate processes by utilizing completely different grammatical resources), but rather is "the indispensable element in the construction of a finite assertive sentence,"[4] a function that can be explicated also by nominal elements: *so even though the nominal phrase lacks a copula, it does not for that reason lack a verb*.

This purely syntactic definition of the verb therefore shows its close relationship with the copulative function. It is in fact completely apparent that the functions Benveniste attributes to the verb are exactly those which Aristotle attributes to the copula: it does not mean anything in itself, if not "some combination (*sýnthesin tina*),"[5] and carries out the function of conferring an assertive character to the sentence by claiming the reality of the subject-predicate conh nection. In Aristotle's theory of judgment, however, the copula "is" combines in itself not only the two functions—synthetic and existential-assertive—which

Benveniste attributed to the verb, but *also* what is the true verbal function for Aristotle: unlike a noun, which is capable of signifying independently of time, the verb (*rhêma*), as he says in *De Interpretatione*, moreover signifies (*prossemáinein*) time.[6] For Aristotle, the verb carries a nominal aspect (it is, taken in itself, a noun), which is its autonomous aspect, and also a copulative aspect, which helps it to constitute a complete sentence and necessarily implies a temporal consignification. In the form "S is P," to which every sentence can be reduced through a paronymous transformation, what in the verb expresses an independent meaning is in fact reduced to a *nominal* predicate, and its temporal consignification is assumed in toto by the copula.[7] Such consignification does not therefore arise suddenly in judgment *because of* the copula, but it is inscribed in the verb ab origine. The copula does nothing but make this relation clear. A purely nominal succession, such as *terrestrial bipedal animal*, is not a sentence: it is one only if there is a verb present in it, at least implicitly. As Aristotle points out: "Every sentence must contain a verb or the tense of a verb. The phrase which defines the species 'man,' if no verb in present, past, or future time be added, is not a sentence."[8] In the copula is found what we can call *the verbal dimension of truth*: there is no *lógos* without the verb, there is no sentence or judgment, and therefore no truth, without temporal consignification.

The various functions or consignifications of the copula are thus not abstractly separable, as if the cohesive and the assertive functions could be present by excluding the temporal function, as happens in the nominal phrase. In particular, the assertive function, which consists in saying the proposed content *is*, that *this* is, avails itself of a deictic element that cannot but introduce a temporal dimension. When one says—or better: when one *understands,* even without saying it explicitly, as is the case with the nominal phrase—that something is, that *this* is, what does one mean, and above all, what *does one do*, if not *refer* a certain content to a moment of time, and thus introduce time as a constitutive element of the utterance of truth itself? What is therefore explicit and manifest in the phrase with the copula is simply implicit in the nominal phrase, which gives to understanding *more* than what appears.[9] Even when it is not materially present, the copulative function is inscribed in judgment at the limit, under the form of an "empty space."[10]

In the wake of Aristotelian doctrine, medieval theologians were at odds over this thorny issue. The atemporality of the proposed content cannot be stated if not in and with time, and this must have some consequences for its truth. In this way M.-D. Chenu formulates the philosophical repercussions of this Aristotelian thesis on the temporal consignification of the copula:

> *Verbum consignificat tempus*. And so a proposition—of which the verb, which expresses the action and its objective and subjective modes, constitutes the foundation—is necessarily connected to time, in its logical structure as well as its truth value. It is not possible to abstract it from time. [. . .] Here enters into play always more explicitly, as an Aristotelian resource, an entire psychology of the activity of the spirit in the act of knowing, against the realism of pure grammar that would tend to establish directly the equivalences between words and things. This equivalence does not exist except in and through the perception of a knowing subject, who therefore necessarily inscribes it onto concepts and onto words. If this knowing subject is an eternal God, it will know these very temporal things in an atemporal manner, with a glance that embraces all time; but if it is a human being, whose intelligence is bound to time in the complexity of judgment and of rational procedures, the most immutable truths must again be dressed in these human ways, and the highest intelligibilities, as with that of faith, will not free it from this mental structure.[11]

Here Chenu says not only that human *knowledge* is temporal, but that truth itself, as inevitably "filtered" by specific human modes of being, cannot be anything but temporal. What is temporal is therefore not so much an aspect of the event under consideration, but the entire judged content. This is the path that will be followed from Kantian critique—whose argumentation seems to be anticipated by these logical-theological discussions—and from Hegelian philosophy, poised to break down even the barrier that critique left between the temporality of human knowledge (the phenomenological dimension) and the in-itself of truth (logic), which entered into history in the same way that the Word was made flesh. In order to see how this can be accomplished, we will now focus preliminarily on responding to another question, rendered urgent by the preceding observations on the presence of the copulative-verbal function in the nominal phrase: can the copula in fact be—not empirically, but in what is given to understanding—totally eliminated from the structure of the sentence? Can a purely *logical,* nominal expression of truth exist (leaving aside completely the problem of its definition)?

The Elimination of the Copula: Truth without Time

The temporal consignification of the copula has a syntactic function that operates alongside its cohesive and assertive functions: through it, the asserted content is related to the temporal situation of whoever asserts it. The copula places the sentence in relation to the speaker, so that if the form "S is P" is the form in which the truth *is said*, it carries with it an unavoidable temporal reference:

> In particular, the phrases Aristotle is apt to have in mind are *temporally indefinite*; they depend on the time of their sentence. They may be said to be relative to the moment at which they are propounded. This relation may be implicit, but it may also be made explicit by the occurrence of such "token-reflexive" expressions as "now" or "at the present moment" in the phrase in question. (Among these we have to count also such expressions as "yesterday" or "tomorrow" where another moment or period of time is specified by reference to the present moment.)[12]

The copula fixes the point of time in respect to which the content of the sentence is modalized. The consignified time is therefore the time of this semantic content in relation to the time of the speaker, the *now* (*nûn*) that constitutes the horizon of every belonging (*hypárchein*), namely, of every existing or non-existing: "I will explain what I mean by saying that it carries with it (*prossemaínei*) the notion of time. 'Health' is a noun, but 'is healthy' is a verb; for besides its proper meaning it indicates the present existence of the state in question (*tò nûn hypárchein*)."[13]

What is temporal is not so much the act described in the sentence, but primarily the whole utterance; not the judged content, but the act of judgment, or more specifically, the act of utterance. What is therefore at stake is not so much time *in* judgment (the time of the event in which the judgment matters), but time that is extra-predicative or—to use a Heideggerian term—existential. Judgment is thus a completely temporal phenomenon: that the copula is essential to it, as that which anchors it to a point in time, means that there is no truth without temporal reference.[14]

It is far too easy to see in Heidegger's ontological hermeneutics a development (through Kant's transcendental revolution), however explicitly defended, of this aspect of the Aristotelian theory of judgment. More surprising, but no less valid, is the rediscovery of its presence in a theory like

Donald Davidson's, which considers utterances as the real truth-bearers, since for him every sentence is always spatially and temporally gathered:

> We could take truth to be a property, not of sentences, but of utterances, or speech acts, or ordered triples of sentences, times, and persons; but it is simplest just to view truth as a relation between a sentence, a person, and a time. Under such treatment, ordinary logic as now read applies as usual, but only to sets of sentences relativized to the same speaker and time.[15]

Davidson's theory unexpectedly appears to be rather close to Aristotle's idea. It is nothing other than the recognition of a status of the expression that Frege's theory had tried in every manner to eliminate. The substitution of the predicative form "S is P" with the function F*x* would in fact have the aim, *above all*, to avoid the copula, the useless and misleading third term. The relation between objects and concepts is for Frege a primitive relation; they constitute two parts of a whole that in turn complete each other, and for that reason there is no need to place a copula or, as Peano did, a sign of belonging between them. Frege's Platonism does not assume Aristotelian predication as a model, which through the copula defines the temporality of belonging (*hypárchein*) between a certain predicate and a subject, but rather consists precisely in Platonic participation (*méthexis*), which points to a constitutive relation of the object that stands completely outside of time. Strictly speaking, the expression F*x* would then be rendered with a nominal phrase: not "Socrates *is* human," but "human Socrates," and this *because for Frege the truth carried by a proposition is an eternal truth.* It does not depend on the fact of being thought or expressed, and in principle has no relation with a speaker or, to put it in Kantian terms, with an "I think"; it is absolute, in itself: thoughts that do not need to be thought, and are expressed in a language that at best is a language of angels.[16]

There is a particular alliance between mathematical logic, as Frege conceives it, and the claim to know the world "in itself"—a claim that Kant branded as dogmatism. The dream that it follows is that of a pure nomination without time, which delivers to us a sort of "brusque catechism" and "a sequence of assertions of truth and rigid definition." The central problem for mathematical logic in its relation with natural language, therefore, is not so much bringing to light the deep logical form that would exist under the superficial grammatical form (a proposal that is less disruptive than we think), but more radically that of eliminating the copula and, with it, every synthetic function—and first of all what every synthetic function carries with it: time. This is a difficulty to which one can attribute the responsibility of having even swept away the reductionist and extensional program of logical empiricism: how in fact are expressions of the form "the quality *q* is at the instant-point *x*; *y*; *z*; *t*," that, according to Rudolf Carnap, ought to constitute the protocol statements for the logical construction of the world, translatable in the language of pure sense-data, of referential entities? As Quine writes in *The Two Dogmas of Empiricism*: "Carnap did not seem to recognize, however, that his treatment of physical objects fell short of reduction not merely through sketchiness, but in principle": the difficulty would be in the fact that "[t]he connective 'is at' remains an added undefined connective; the canons counsel us in its use but not in its elimination."[17]

This comment is remarkably similar to what Heidegger accuses Husserl of when he shows the impossibility of reducing what is *understood* in language to what is perceived. By taking the sentence "this chair is yellow and upholstered" as an example, Heidegger inquires:

> Our question is whether this sentence finds its complete fulfillment in what is perceived. Is every intention within the full intending and utterance perceptually demonstrable in the subject matter? [. . .] I can see the chair, its being-*upholstered* and its being-*yellow* but I shall never in all eternity see the "this," "is," "and" as I see the chair. There is in the full perceptual sentence a *surplus of intentions* whose determination cannot be borne by the simple perception of the subject matter.[18]

As with Quine's objection to Carnap, it is not only a question of completion; rather, it deals with an excess of meaning that, in the reduction of the intention to what is perceived, is presupposed but not perceived. What is at stake here is the meaning of the copula, of the "is," the symbol of every connection, of every synthesis. In such a case, this could be a further reason to speak of what Heidegger calls the "*oblivion* of Being," an underlying understanding that is, however, covered and not perceived as such.

The meaning of Being can be forgotten; but can this forgetting result in its complete elimination from language? The copula, as we were saying, expresses through its modulations the time of the asserted event *in reference to* the time of the utterance; in this way it inevitably carries with it a reference to the speaker, and by that, all that belongs to the speaker. The interpretative turn brought by Davidson to analytic philosophy, which implicates a broad reference to intentions, propositional attitudes and modalities intrinsic to expression, has done nothing less than open a passage across the imperceptible breach represented by the "is." Through the "is," in fact, what Heidegger calls "understanding" enters forcefully onto the scene: the modality of being-there of the subject of the utterance, the real *consignificatum* of the copula.

Signifying the Non-objectual: Synthesis and Time

Kant's "Copernican Revolution" introduces a radical change in perspective in the theory of judgment. In fact, predicates no longer revolve around a logical subject; instead, the entire judgment revolves around the transcendental Subject. The pivot point of this revolution is the copula: through the copula, the *truth in itself* of the judgment inevitably becomes a *truth for us*, and only for this reason is it an *objective* truth. The copula designates this relation, this transcendental "*for*" without which any judgment would not be possible:

> This is what is intended by the copula 'is.' It is employed to distinguish the objective unity of given representations from the subjective. It indicates their relation to original apperception, and its *necessary unity*. It holds good even if the judgment is itself empirical.[19]

The judgment is objective as long as the copula expresses a *necessary* connection to the "I think," a connection that is not limited to the mere relation by which a certain *this* is relative to an empirical consciousness. The copula expresses the transcendental relation to the "I think" as a necessary relation so that every *this* can subsist within *a* possible experience: Kant transfers the synthetic consignification (and with it, the temporal one) from the logical-grammatical realm to the transcendental realm. Kant's untiring effort was to thematize a field that overflows the field of formal logic by demonstrating that it is not possible to extend the traditional understanding of the relation internal to judgment—as a merely logical relation of subsumption or of inherence between the subject and predicate—to the transcendental relation. His declared dissatisfaction with the way logicians understood judgment (as "representation of a relation between two concepts"), with which he opens §19 of the *Critique of Pure Reason*, is due not only to the fact that this definition rests *within* judgment and thus is suitable only for categorical judgments, but above all to the fact that it "does not determine in what the asserted *relation* consists."[20] The traditional understanding of the relation between subject and predicate in fact applies only to categorical and not to hypothetical or disjunctive judgments, which entail a relation *between* judgments and not between the subject and the predicate. Here is the reason for yet again realizing the difference between Kant's notion of the categories as basically extra-apophantic forms of synthesis, and Aristotle's as intra-apophantic forms of synthesis. The schema of the transcendental conception of judgment in Kant could thus be the following:

S is P | "I think"	the intra-apophantic relation is founded, by means of the copula, on a transcendental relation to the "I think."

The vertical line represents the constitutive act of judgment that is the function, through the categories, of the "I think." Every category, therefore, or every form of synthesis present in a judgment, of which the copula is only the eminent form, cannot for Kant indicate a mere logical relation, but indicates a logical relation *by means* of the transcendental relation to the "I think," thanks to which the whole of experience is constituted as a unity. And so, in hypothetical judgment, the particles "if . . . then . . . " (the symbol →) do not represent anything related to an object, but refer to the "I think" and find their ground in it.

Therefore, the relation represented by the copula is above all a transcendental relation, a relation to the "I think" that is made immanent in judgment (in experience) but does not wholly belong to judgment. ("But though all our knowledge begins *with* experience, it does not follow that it all arises *out of* experience.")[21] Far from being constituted through an elision of the copula, and thus of what it designates—the relation to a cogito—the objectivity in transcendentalism rests exactly on the necessity of this relation. But precisely because it is necessary, it is in truth more general and more fundamental than a solely accidental and subjective relation. In order to avoid every subjective relation, and therefore also the transcendental one, Frege's objectivism believed it was able to avoid every relation between the subject and the predicate. That logical language should in this way be reduced by right (if not by fact) to the nominal syntax (in which case it would be more correct to interpret F*x* as "human Socrates" and not as "Socrates is human") is a requirement prescribed by the very elision of the copulative relation.

In Fregean ideography an equivalent of the copula is the sign of judgment, or that vertical line placed before the horizontal line or sign of content, which in its turn precedes the propositional sign: |-F*x*. Russell rightly observes that the horizontal line does not express a true copulative relation, but the simple object of representation or the mere content of thinking ("the cold of the wind"), while it is the vertical line that indicates a copulative relation, and therefore a true act of judgment: the idea, namely, that a certain content is to be assumed as true or false ("the wind is cold"). In the wake of Meinong, Russell then understands this distinction as two different modes of relating to the same object: the "is" would eventually introduce a difference in meaning, and this is the reason why in the end he claims that the sign of judgment cannot be considered a component—like the predicates—of what is represented. The tacit premise, as noted by Eva Picardi, is that for any sign belonging to a logical proposition there corresponds a *constituent* external to the proposition.[22] This vertical line, equivalent to the copula that for Kant is the symbol of pure apperception and for Aristotle consignifies time, would therefore allude to something that is not an object and that as such finds no full representation in the proposition.

But does the fact that the vertical line does not correspond to any element external to the proposition necessarily mean that it is also something *non-constitutive*?

> There is a subtle irony in the objections which Frege and Peano, both passionate followers of the Leibnizian idea of a *lingua characteristica*, joined to the terms of their inquiry: what instills life in the signs of the ideography is not completely expressible from within. Nonetheless, the search for the discerning logical notation is neither futile, nor chimerical. Indirectly the ideography allows it to circumscribe what evades genuine symbolic representation: the tendency toward truth that motivates thinking, fixed on the page by the vertical line, which is a truly *sui generis* sign.[23]

If the vertical sign of judgment represents something, it is the *tendency* of thought toward the truth; is this not a way to designate the *transcendental* relation, that "metaphysical need" of truth that constitutes a natural disposition of humanity, the indication of human finitude (of human temporality) and the foundation—however equally *constitutive*—of the objectivity of knowledge? Does the vertical sign, or the copula, therefore not allude—in a necessarily *vertical* way, a way that transcends judgment—to that place that makes every truth about the world possible, and that Heidegger calls the "there" of Dasein, or "disclosedness"?

These questions trace a line of development in the reflection on judgment that offers an alternative to the one of the *lingua characteristica*, in the sense that it tries to grasp exactly what this cannot represent, and for that reason avails itself of a different logic, a transcendental logic. As Kant clarifies, it deals with the "that" (*dass*) and the "how" (*wie*) of the object, constituted in a judgment. That the term "judgment" in Kant is synonymous with the term "proposition" is not an error that Frege would have to correct, and this is because for Kant there is no proposition without a transcendental relation to the Subject, namely, without the copula. The Fregean proposition is not a judgment because the functional expression F*x* (pure angelic thinking) has, or claims to have, a nominal constitution, confirmed by the fact that for Frege propositions are names of the true and the false: by having to express the truth *in themselves*, they cannot signify that truth other than independently of time. But if the form "S is P" is the form in which the object is originarily given, then there is no truth in itself that is not also a truth for us, since the "is"—which in general represents every synthetic and cohesive function—is ineliminable from the deep structure of the proposition and signifies exactly the *for us* of its truth. Without the relation that it signifies, there is surely no experience, and thus no object, but only "anonymous" sense-data.

When one speaks of "transcendental," one is still taken to mean something constitutive, and thus—the consequence seems inevitable—something atemporal: the logicization of Kant's aesthetics by the neo-Kantians is ultimately a sort of misunderstanding of Kant's intentions. In aesthetics Kant saw, on the contrary, the limit of the complete intellectualization of experience. Such a limit is in the temporal, and not the logical, nature of every synthesis, including even the supreme synthesis that unifies experience, the function of the "I think." Kant himself, however, according to Heidegger's interpretation found in *Kant and the Problem of Metaphysics*, would not have seen completely that the transcendental relation grounding the apophantic (synthetic) relation is temporal. Such a hypothesis would place the Kantian conception of the copula in the wake of the Aristotelian tradition that goes back to *De interpretatione*; Heidegger notes this by commenting on the passage where Aristotle introduces the temporal signification of the copula:

> From this brief yet quite fundamental interpretation of the meaning of being qua "is" in Aristotle, we shall take three things: [1.] The guiding

> meaning of the "is" is *meaning-in-addition* (*Dazu-bedeuten*). It is not an independent meaning, such as the naming of something. Rather, in its meaningful function as such, the meaning of being and "is" is already related to something that is. [2.] In that which means-in-addition, the "is" means *synthesis, connectedness, unity*. [3.] The "is" does not mean *pragma, does not mean some matter* or thing. Precisely this same interpretation of the "is" was provided, centuries later, by Kant, perhaps without his knowing this place in Aristotle, yet while being guided by the tradition, which he then managed to grasp more profoundly in this interpretation of the copula.[24]

Paradoxically, it is the same distinction between Aesthetics and Logic, between the forms of intuition and the categories, or between the temporal synthesis and the intellectual synthesis, that still does not allow Kant to see in the copula the phenomenon in which *both* of these functions of synthesis are grounded and find their foundation, namely, to see that intimate connection between *consignificatio temporis* and *consignificatio compositionis*. However, it happens rather clearly, as Hegel notes, in the role attributed to the transcendental imagination, the abyss which Kant, according to Heidegger, did not risk examining, and that Heidegger himself attempted in an Analytic of Dasein, that is, an ontology of finite, temporal being.

The Speculative Proposition: The Time of Knowing

The anchoring of truth to a transcendental condition (the "I think") or to the existence of a finite being (Dasein) constitutes an itinerary within which an important, and in many ways alternative, stage is represented by the Hegelian conception of judgment. The structure of judgment, which links the subject and the predicate without exposing the movement of their identity, fixed through the copula, is for Hegel not adequate to express truth, as this is not a mere result, but the result together with its becoming.[25] Here arises the need to explain this movement of truth, an objective movement which is anterior and correlative to the subjective movement of knowing. Being and thought, truth and certainty, reality and consciousness, subject and object, or even positive and negative, are taken in a movement whose dialectic is given precisely by the impossibility of splitting them, of separating them completely. This movement of knowing *and* of truth is not demonstrated by the copula, which fixes only a moment within that movement, but by the syllogism, which gives substance to the mediation that it supposes:

> Still, the rational or, as Kant calls it, the a priori nature of this judgment, the absolute identity as the mediating concept (*Mittelbegriff*) manifests itself, not in the judgment, but in the [syllogistic] inference. In the judgment the absolute identity is merely the copula "is," without consciousness. It is the difference whose appearance prevails in the judgment itself [. . .]. The copula is not something thought, something cognized; on the contrary it expresses precisely our non-cognizance of the rational. What comes to the fore and enters consciousness is only the product, i.e., the subject and predicate as terms of the antithesis. Only these terms are posited as object of thought in the form of judgment, and not their being one.[26]

The *temporal* fixedness of the copula transfers to the subjective side—the side of knowing—the fixedness of truth that in the nominal phrase regards its objective content. Established truths are expressed in judgment: "[t]his concept relies on truths which are taken for granted and which it sees no need to re-examine; it just lays them down, and believes it is entitled to assert them, as well as to judge and pass phrase by appealing to them."[27] They are exempt from experience:

> In place of the long process of culture towards genuine philosophy, a movement as rich as it is profound, through which Spirit achieves knowledge, we are offered as quite equivalent either direct revelations from heaven, or the sound common sense that has never laboured over, or informed itself regarding other knowledge or genuine philosophy; and we are assured that these are quite as good substitutes as some claim chicory is for coffee.[28]

These are the truths that pass themselves off as "common sense," and that "have long since been available in catechisms or in popular sayings, etc."[29] They are truths that claim to be believed because of their merely affirmative character as a "belief," as with those truths of faith that are stated in judgments, namely in the form of a division (*Ur-teil*, judgment, is the "originary separation" for Hegel) that, in unifying the subject and the predicate, at the same time separates the judged content from knowing. The copula is the crossing point of this "diairetic synthesis," which makes faith the very perspective of the finite, separated being: faith (truth not known, and thus accepted as it is given) and intelligence (the static nature of the conceptual definition) are therefore correlative perspectives for Hegel, to which he opposes his conception of the concept as life, dynamic unity of content and form, self-movement, and spirit.

The Kantian conception, which Hegel still considers bound to this dimension of faith, since it denies the possibility that reason can *know* the in-itself, is for Hegel an overcoming, albeit partial, of the traditional conception of judgment. Kant rightly sees that the relation between the transcendental Subject and its contents cannot be reduced to the relation between the subject and predicate, namely, that the intra-apophantic relation cannot become the model for understanding the extra-apophantic relation—an extrapolation that had led Descartes to define the Subject as a *res cogitans*, as though its contents would subsist in relation to it as the predicates are in relation to the substance. But, by keeping the "fixity" of the relation internal to the judgment, Kant inevitably extended it also to the transcendental relation and thereby conceived the transcendental Subject as the "fixed point" upon which the variable multiplicity of experience is anchored: "this subject constitutes the basis to which the content is attached, and upon which the movement runs back and forth."[30]

In the ratiocinating or intellectual manner of understanding judgment, thinking in fact moves from the subject to its predicate; but it either rediscovers the substantial element in the predicate itself (as in the relation of subsumption) or it rediscovers it in the subject (as in the relation of inherence). In both cases, the movement stops on the one side or the other, "held by such a heaviness." The Kantian "I" is, according to Hegel, tied to its contents by a relation similar to the one of inherence: "Here, that Subject is replaced by the knowing 'I' itself, which links the Predicates with the Subject holding them."[31] The copula is the bond of this relation.

To destroy such a form of judgment, which "involves the distinction of Subject and Predicate,"[32] signifies for Hegel destroying *this mode of understanding* their relation. This is possible by doing what Kant refused to do, namely, moving the whole of the transcendental relation (which is reducible neither to a substantial relation nor to one of inherence) *within* judgment, moving consciousness and its negative dimension within judgment, turning it into the true mover of reality: judgment speaks reality but must at the same time reflect, speculatively, the movement of knowing. The speculative or philosophical proposition,

> since it *is* a proposition, leads one to believe that the usual subject-predicate relation obtains, as well as the usual attitude towards knowing. But the philosophical content destroys this attitude and this opinion. We learn by experience that we meant something other than we meant to mean; and this correction of our meaning compels our knowing to go back to the proposition, and understand it in some other way.[33]

This movement of return does not belong to, and cannot be displayed in, a simple judgment, which therefore is not the adequate form of truth: it is shown only in a dialectical-syllogistic concatenation of judgments. Such a speculative dimension, which implies the ideal reversibility of the temporal progression, is the temporality of spirit. For Hegel, spirit is in fact "return," and in this sense is the negation of the negation. This idea, on the one hand, keeps Hegel within a tradition that conceived of the movement of knowing and of reality as grounded upon an identity that must ultimately be expressed, recovered, restored (we must pay attention for this to the forms of the disjunctive syllogism, which for Hegel constitutes the supreme form of the real);[34] on the other hand, this conception distances Hegel from the irreversible, *finite* temporality, which has its point of non-reflectiveness and asymmetry in the event of death.[35]

The exposition of knowing is therefore inevitably compelled to transgress the form of judgment, to destroy in the first place the temporal fixedness of the copula, which couples the judged content to a *moment* of time and holds it fast as a base in relation to its determinations. The Subject has nevertheless to be conceived as *the becoming of the object*: "[the Self] is not a passive Subject inertly supporting the Accidents; it is, on the contrary, the self-moving Notion which takes its determinations back into itself."[36] If the ratiocinating manner is limited to express the true as substance, Hegel intends to complete this program speculatively by demonstrating that it is, equally, the Subject.[37]

The Hegelian conception of judgment is the attempt to overcome every position of truth that is expressed in the form of a *thesis* without movement: the assertion of identity (to which the content of the nominal phrase is reduced, as we have seen) could in fact be considered immune from any temporal consignification. Hegel, however, wants to negate the possibility that any truth could be expressed in such a way: truth is experience, in which every judgment, and even the position of identity, *becomes* a knowing. Hegel qualifies this movement of thinking, which is elevated to knowing through experience, as *objective*, an aspect which can lead to a confrontation with the objectivity that Frege gives to thought.[38] Nevertheless, Frege's conception of objectivity is achieved at the cost of excluding knowledge from the object, while for Hegel it is precisely knowledge that *constitutes* the object, which is not something immobile or atemporal, according to the specifically Heraclitian torsion that Hegel impresses upon the Parmenidean identity of being and thought. In Frege the copula disappears in order to achieve the atemporality of the logical object; in Hegel it disappears in order to unlink knowledge from its temporal fixedness (a fixedness that crystallizes the judged content by turning it into a content of faith). Time does not simply belong to the phenomenological movement of the individual consciousness, which on its itinerary would discover a truth already given, but belongs intrinsically to the manifestation of spirit, to its self-exposition through its self-movement. From this point of view, there could be no position further from the Fregean one. What they share is the appearing and disappearing of the copula in the exposition of knowledge, whose gap constitutes the vital space of finite being.

From Time to *Consignificatio Existentiae*

Up to this point, the interpretation of the copula has remained for the most part contained within a fundamentally gnoseological thematic. To know is to judge, and what matters in judgment is truth. Nevertheless, any gnoseology must face up to the ontological question: the necessary—even if it is not sufficient—condition of the truth of a judgment is the existence of the subject. To say that a judgment is true, therefore, is the same as asserting that the subject, about which one claims it is such and such, exists. *Aliquid est.* Implicitly, therefore, in a true judgment the copula is loaded with an ulterior meaning—an existential one, on which its assertive function depends. That Fx is true means above all that $\exists x = a$, such that Fa.[39]

For the theories of denotation, the presupposition of truth is thus the existence of objects corresponding to names: naming, as a grammatical function specifically disposed to denote such entities, therefore assumes a primary role. The noun is what is capable of signifying independently of time. As a result, whatever is said exists because it is denoted by a noun: it is in itself, or even in its essence, atemporal. Only its accidents are temporal. From that it ought to follow that time, in itself, cannot be named.[40] The idea that the copula—which in effect is neither a name nor a term—is what signifies time is thus a direct result of this theorem. The form of this signification escapes from the logic of denotation, and even from logic tout court.

Descartes (who had transmitted to Kant the definition of judgment as the act of synthesis and of separation between ideas) transferred this logic—which understands the existing entity as the correlate of a name—to the epistemological problematic of a foundation for knowledge in the conscious Subject. In this way the existing subject, the *sum* of the cogito, has been thought as a substance. Kant's critique of the substantialization of the "I think" thus demonstrates his full awareness that no res can be deduced from the "is" of judgment, which acts as the transcendental foundation of the objectivity of knowledge. The copula does not name any reality (as Heidegger says in his commentary on *De interpretatione*), and it does not have an autonomous meaning, as happens with names; thus, it does not signify *a thing*.

The existing signified by the copula is not substance. In the wake of Kant, Heidegger rescues this consequence from the transcendental deduction, which now takes on a peculiar ontological twist, since it makes explicit the consignification of Dasein present in every judgment, that *ego sum* implied in every cogito. If a true and objective judgment implicates, as the condition of its possibility, an existence, this is above all the existence of that *x* on which such objectivity, or even the "I think," is founded:

> What is here the unknown = X, which gives support to the understanding when it believes that it can discover outside the concept A a predicate B foreign to this concept, which it yet at the same time considers to be connected with it? It cannot be experience, because the suggested principle has connected the second representation with the first, not only with greater universality, but also with the character of necessity, and therefore completely *a priori* and on the basis of mere concepts.[41]

The copula, as the expression of the objectivity of consciousness, attests to such a subject; for Heidegger, it attests to such a subject as Dasein. Judgment, and therefore truth, is anchored to Dasein through the copula. This is the meaning of the phrase, "'There *is' truth only in so far as Dasein is and so long as Dasein is.*"[42] If the transcendental dimension, the condition of truth, cannot be a component of the proposition, it is however its "horizon of possibility," the opening, the "there" in which Dasein and world co-belong. In their *necessary* relation stands the authentic form of the a priori synthesis: the "is" of judgment expresses, through its temporal consignification, this necessary condition of truth as truth *for* us, namely, for a finite being. The condition of truth for judgment is therefore not *aliquid est*—the formula in which the realism of scholastic metaphysics is summed up; above all, as the true a priori, this condition is *aliquis est.*

The Aristotelian conception of *consignificatio temporis*, as we have seen, was already leading in this direction. The time signified in the judgment is a function of the being-now of the subject of the utterance. That means: before being true, namely, before involving the existence of the object denoted by the logical subject, the judgment involves the existence of the subject of the utterance. The fact that this argumentation is focused on the *consignificatio temporis* is a guiding thread that ties together the Aristotelian doctrine, the Kantian conception of judgment as the function of the synthetic unity of apperception, and Heidegger's ontological hermeneutics.

For Heidegger, therefore, it is a matter of rethinking the problematic of judgment in an ontological key. The "is" does not express a simple relation between the subject and the predicate, but the "There" of Dasein. The foundation of the synthetic and temporal consignifications of the "is" lies in its *consignificatio existentiae.*

> [H]ow far on the other hand the concept of "judgment" has (by a remarkable counter-thrust) worked its way into the ontological problematic, is shown by the phenomenon of the *copula* [. . .] But if the formal characteristics of "relating" and "binding" can contribute nothing phenomenally towards the structural analysis of the *logos* as subject-matter, then in the long run the phenomenon to which we allude by the term "copula" has nothing to do with a bond or binding. The interpretation of the "is," whether it be expressed in its own right in the language or indicated in the verbal ending, leads us therefore into the context of problems belonging to the existential analytic, if assertion and the understanding of Being are existential possibilities for the Being of Dasein itself.[43]

Hermeneutic ontology thus leads to an overcoming of the boundaries of the gnoseological problematic, which was limited to the problem of truth, and moves rather in the direction of the problem of sense, that is, of understanding. In fact, what attests to Dasein is not only the synthesis of the possible object, that is, the judgment that presents an object of experience; Dasein's "presence" is actually implicated in *every* synthesis. Even in the judgment without an object, one that is contradictory and absurd, and thus *logically* meaningless, one that could barely be called a "judgment" because it lacks any value as knowledge, it is possible, and indeed we must, presuppose an existence. Even in the midst of delirium and foolishness, or in incoherent discourse—in the absence of judgment—the synthesis, however minimal it is, attests to the fact of an existence, a "There," and therefore a sense, however indescribable in terms of good logical sense, that is still reduced to the constitution of a possible *object*. This phenomenon is what I have called elsewhere "radical understanding."[44] A minimal understanding inheres even in the most indecipherable inscriptions or phrases, which does not concern their content, but rather their *form*, their very condition of possibility as "inscriptions" and phrases. The simple fact that they could be recognized as indecipherable or incomprehensible carries the recognition of their relation with a Dasein that has produced them. "Radical understanding" (an expression that clearly recalls those of radical translation and radical interpretation, attributed to Quine and Davidson) regards this minimal and absolutely unerasable content, which must be understood in every object that is recognized as actually or potentially meaningful, and that consists in the formal relation of such an object to the subject of its production, and even to a Dasein. It is Dasein, inasmuch as it *is* in the world, and not the object, that first of all has meaning:

> Meaning is an *existentiale* of Dasein, not a property attaching to entities, laying "behind" them, or floating somewhere as an "intermediate domain." Dasein only "has" meaning, so far as the disclosedness of Being-in-the-world can be "filled in" by the entities discoverable in that disclosedness.[45]

The *constitutive* role of time in the expression of truth in a judgment is due to the fact that the foundation—namely, the subject—of every judgment (Dasein) is temporal. An eternal truth, without time, would thus not have any meaning for us. It would have to elide the condition of possibility of judgment, would have to cancel out in principle what we, in fact, understand in a judgment, through whatever synthesis, whether it is or is not expressed, and which we identify grammatically with the copula. This understanding is not exterior and successive, and thus in principle unnecessary for the expression of truth, but rather constitutive of what *for us* is true. Through the "There" of Dasein, *every* truth, even those that concern presumed atemporal entities, is *temporal* in a radical way. The sense of being *in general* is what cannot *not* be understood whenever one says "is"—namely, time.

Chapter 3

The Experience of Truth as the Experience of Time

The Form of Truth: Deixis and the Elliptical Character of Judgment

The Heideggerian rebuttal to the traditional conception of truth as correspondence or equivalence between the mind and the thing was given with a more profound and originary understanding in mind. That model is rejected not because it is not "adequate"—which would produce a performative contradiction, since it would be used in order to challenge it—but because it is derivative. This clarification helps to dispel a misunderstanding to which the Heideggerian notion of truth was often exposed—namely, that it would completely reject the notion of correspondence or adequation, along with its staid and longstanding tradition, in favor of a much more inconsistent, mystical, and rather vague notion of truth. In reality, Heidegger himself recognized the legitimacy of the conception of truth as adequation, to the point of saying that if it has been around for this long, it must certainly contain in itself something of positive value.[1]

The thoughts developed in the preceding chapters give us some indication of this. The passage from the predicative realm to the antepredicative realm of the existence of Dasein is certainly required by the fact that if there is a sentence, there is also someone who utters it; if there is affirmation or negation—the conditions of truth, for Aristotle—in judgment there is also a verb,[2] which inevitably carries a *consignificatio temporis*, or even a deictic coordination of judgment with respect to the subject of the utterance, to Dasein. It is not surprising that the term "Dasein" (which also signifies "to exist") is a deictic term, no more or less than the expression "I think" that designates the transcendental subject. This "originary deixis" constitutes the point of temporal and spatial coordination of every predication and of every judgment, and therefore of truth.

The deictic reference of the sentence to the moment of its utterance introduces a sort of "transcendental occasionality" in the conception of truth: occasional sentences are those that do not completely contain their meaningful content, as in the case of "it is raining today." These include all of the sentences that entail deictic references, such as the spatiotemporal adverbs and the first and second person pronouns "I" and "you." This type of sentence is "incomplete": it can—at least apparently—be completed by making its deictic references explicit in the sentence, for example in the form "it is raining in Paris on May 5, 2010." The question, however, is whether such a chronological clarification really eliminates them: in fact, how is one to define "May 5, 2010" or the place in which one finds Paris? The dating is only apparently independent of the speaker; in fact there is no way to determine the year zero, from which the year 2010 is determined, if not as that year which corresponds to *2010 years ago* (that is, by beginning with today, which is the time of the speaker). There is no way to determine the place in which one finds Paris, if not by starting from the place in which *I* find myself now. No temporal or spatial reference is possible without referring in a more or less direct manner to the position of the speaker, unless space and time are conceived as absolutes, as *sensorium dei*. Thus, if every spatiotemporal reference always, sooner or later, leads back to the deixis of the speaker—and namely to the particular manner in which the speaker is grammaticalized in the assertion—then every assertion is always essentially occasional, that is, *incomplete*, and characterized by an essential and insuperable elliptical feature.

This elliptical feature[3] is inherent to the grammatical or syntactical structuring of judgment, that is, inherent to its *form*. That the judged *content* is "eternally" true does not preclude this formal structure; what is unavoidably temporal—because it is marked by an unerasable deixis—is the form of truth (equivalent to what Kant would call "the form of experience"), namely, its transcendental condition of possibility. The very form of truth is thus temporal. Newton's laws were not true before he discovered them; however, this does not mean that they were false,[4] but only that they did not yet have the possible form of being true—they were not yet *formulated* in a judgment. And this formulation happened for the first time with Newton. All of this is equal to saying that the bearers of truth (or: what can be true or false), as we have seen in chapter 2, are neither propositions nor sentences, but utterances or speech acts. The "identical and immutable relation" between presumed propositions in themselves and the state of affairs does not exclude its inscription on the background of a temporality expressed as the deictic reference to the subject of the utterance.

Correspondence and Metaphysics

The correspondence theory of truth, far from being false, is for Heidegger a derivative formulation that must be scrutinized in its ontological presuppositions; and far from offering a solution, it is only the posing of a problem.[5] The correspondence theory "conceals" a more radical dimension of truth, one that remains in oblivion. The aim is not to arrive at a different conception of truth, but rather to explicate a concept that is more originary than alternative, and that in fact is presupposed by the very idea of adequation. As we have seen, one of these presuppositions is that of the *consignificatio existentiae* of the subject of the utterance, mediated by the *consignificatio temporis*. But this path, which leads to the individuation of the transcendental form in time, can be followed in another way: not *a parte subjecti*, that is, in the direction of the subject of the utterance, but *a parte objecti*, that is, in the direction of the denoted object. This path is no longer grammatical but phenomenological. Because there is adequation between the mind or a sentence and things, these must in fact be preliminarily manifest: "The proposition is true in so far as it *conforms* to something already true, i.e., to a being that is unhidden in its being. Truth in this sense of *correctness* presupposes unhiddenness."[6] In order to indicate this diverse conception of truth, Heidegger employs, as is well known, the Greek word *alétheia*.

We can understand this word in two different ways, distinguished by its phenomenological meaning (the manifestation of an essence) or its ontological meaning (the manifestation of an existence). The first meaning, even before Husserlian phenomenology, found a precise theorization in medieval thought, by which *verum* is a predicate that is attributed to every entity precisely as it simply *is that which is* (*verum est id quod est*). It is the reason for which we say that truths, as Thomas Aquinas observed, belong not only to sentences, but also to the objects themselves, as when we speak of "true gold" or a "true friend." In this way, truth tends to be reduced to a tautological relation, which is anterior to the *ratio veritatis*, namely, to the relation of correspondence or adequation, a relation that to the pure tautology of "a = a" *adds* something else—namely, the relation with the intellect.[7]

In my opinion, the profound meaning of Heideggerian *alétheia* does not reside in this phenomenological-essentialist view. It alludes not so much to the manifestation of something in what it is, but to the fact that something is. It then has an ontological valence rather than a phenomenological one. The so-called metaphysical-realism ends up confounding these two aspects, or making them coincide, because for it the simple fact of existing also implies the full identification of something. To exist is thus to be exactly this or that: *no entity without identity*. For Heidegger, on the other hand, the two realms remain distinct, and the notion of *alétheia* is precisely what maintains that distinction.

Both the transcendental conception of truth (according to which every entity, for the very fact of being present to consciousness, is true) and also the realist conception (according to which every entity has its essential identity), which together define the phenomenological conception of truth, do not yet fully capture and thus partly obscure the meaning of Greek experience contained in the term *alétheia* to which Heidegger alludes, because they primarily express the experience of a positivity, of a particular being that, as manifest, is present. In a certain sense, phenomenology remains anchored in a positive conception (although not positivistic) of the phenomenon, precisely because the experience that it describes is completely the experience of being as a positive given—present and "in itself." It characterizes the intuitionism of phenomenology, which to a certain extent also seems to be present in Heidegger, especially where he insists on the fundamentality of *aísthesis* as "it is encountered by life insofar as life stands toward its world."[8] Nevertheless, the way in which he conceives the manifestation—the phenomenon—changes radically.

This can be appreciated through the way that Heidegger understands the German word *Wesen* (essence), which constitutes a fundamental term in the phenomenological theorization of the phenomenon. He understands *Wesen* not in a substantive sense, but in a verbal sense. *Wesen* is in fact an ancient form of the verb "to be" in German, of which traces remain in the past participle (*gewesen*) and the imperfect (*war*) forms of *sein*. It means "to persist," not in the form of atemporality, but in the sense of duration and process. The truth of something is its essence (*Wesen*) in the sense that its enduring begins at an initial moment when it *west*, appears. The idea of time, and thus the idea of finitude, is implicated in the duration. *Wesen* therefore does not express merely atemporal or ahistorical present-ness, but *perdurance* in time. It refers back to an initial moment, to an "inaugural event" nominated by the alpha privative in the word *alétheia*. As Franco Volpi writes,

> by articulating the understanding of being and of truth in such a way—according to the "dynamic" of concealment and unconcealment, hiddenness and manifestation, truth and non-truth, affirmativity and

> negativity—Heidegger takes on the problem of the event of being from the point of view of radical finitude.[9]

This "dynamic," as Volpi calls it, is no longer a fact of intuition (the reference to a specific given) but of understanding (the relation between two moments or elements).

A certain substantialistic reading of the Heideggerian concept of *alétheia* leads to the thought that the unconcealment regards a *quid* that was at first hidden and that now is instead made manifest. This reading of *alétheia*, which could be defined as "exegetical," presupposes the existence of a reserve of hidden meanings that truth is tasked with revealing and bringing to light. In my view, the meaning of truth as *alétheia* does not reside in these "mystical" reasons, but in a more formal characterization that emerges from its lexical construction, that is, in the differentiality expressed by the alpha privative, which confers on this word the sense of a change, of a transformation internal to experience. *Alétheia* does not so much refer to experience that reveals a once obscured content, as it does to an experience of transformation. What is of importance is not *what* is revealed, or even that *something* is revealed, but the fact *that* this happened, that a change is *verified*.[10] Its meaning is one of a historical eventuality, the condition of appearing for some determinate content. As has been noted, it regards the manifestation of an existence rather than of an essence.

Beyond Parmenides: Excess as Future and Anticipation

The essence of truth is therefore not some universal concept—and it is doubtful that a similar definition could ever be given—but its very happening; it is truth not as presence but as happening and, as such, the installation of a difference. Its ontological significance consists in the fact that it is completely one with its temporal dimension. This is what Heidegger demonstrates, beginning with some gnoseological considerations, in his 1931–32 course, *The Essence of Truth*, the second part of which is dedicated to Plato's *Theaetetus*. The turning point of the dialogue, to which Heidegger pays particular attention, is a moment in which, after having shown the untenability of the thesis according to which knowledge (*episteme*) is sensation (*aísthesis*), the need for a different definition is addressed (*Theaet.* 185a). The difficulty of reducing knowledge to sensation appears as the difficulty of synthesizing the multiple and often opposed terms that are furnished by the senses: how, after all, are sounds *and* colors—all of which we say, however, *are*—unified in a singular representation of an object? What they have in common is already the fact that they "are," but evidently this cannot be a given that originates in simple sensation, which can only furnish a determinate quality. The problem is classic: it deals with the problem of synthesis and its *excessive* character in respect to simple sensation, a "more" that is necessarily implicated in their very numerability, even if diverse elements were not qualitatively unified in a precise representation of the object.

> The one and the other are not already as such two; we must first add "and" as a "plus." Every plus is an and, but not every and is a plus. A plurality is still not something countable as such, it is not yet a so-and-so-many. Both must first be given *as beings*, one and the other, and then we *can* take them as two, although we need not do so.[11]

The "more" that is there in the perceived, and that above all allows everything to be apprehended as "being," by demonstrating that "being" is its common element (*koinón*, *Theaet.* 185b), is a sort of excess that, in Plato's analysis, necessarily requires the overcoming of the Protegorean anthropology that reduces the human being to mere sensation. The sign of this overcoming is the postulation (almost a sort of "transcendental deduction" *ante litteram*) of the soul, thanks to which the senses are no longer the subject of knowing (that which knows), but only the means (*órgana*) of knowing (that through which—*dià*—one knows, *Theaet.* 184c ff.). The soul is the faculty predisposed to grasp the excess that sensation is not capable of grasping and that is presented as a certain form of synthesis (*Theaet.* 184d).

What Plato thematizes here could be expressed in Kantian terms as "the condition of possibility of experience." In the definition of knowledge this is a crucial point, for as the preceding arguments have demonstrated, it is not possible to limit knowledge to the *hic et nunc*, namely, to the absolutely discontinuous temporality of sensation. Knowledge is such even when a sensation is no longer present. It is knowledge, whether it is in reference to the past (what I saw yesterday is still true today, *Theaet.* 163c) or to the future (the doctor knows how to predict the effect of a certain medicine, and for this reason he is considered wise, *Theaet.* 178c). This condition therefore supposes a temporality in which it is possible to hold together the past, the present, and the future; or even, it is one in which *past, present, and future are possible* as such. The temporality of knowledge is necessarily that of the *continuum* made possible by the synthesis.

This is the function of the soul. The two analogies that are presented in *Theaetetus*—the wax tablet and the aviary—have the aim of highlighting the fundamental relation between the soul and memory, that is, with time. Without the possibility of holding, without the ability to bring one's consciousness into the present, there would be no knowledge. The second analogy, that of the aviary, above all, introduces a distinction that, under the appearance of an epistemological problem, brings about an ontological differentiation that is rather important. The distinction between "having" and "possessing" allows one to say that it is possible to possess some knowledge without having it in actual form, as in the case of the person who "has bought a coat and owns it, but is not wearing it." In this case "we should say he possesses it without having it about him" (*Theaet.* 197b). Obviously, this distinction refers to the Platonic doctrine according to which knowledge is *anamnesis*; but, more simply, it indicates that knowledge presupposes memory, that is, the capacity to produce a temporal *continuum* that goes beyond the punctuality of sensation. This distinction constitutes the true coup de grâce against Parmenideism, whose logic still guides the arguments that Theaetetus makes in favor of his first definition of knowledge as sensation.

This logic is briefly resumed at the beginning of the discussion of the second thesis (knowledge is true opinion, *alethès dóxa*). They decide, in fact, to pose the question by considering the tougher alternative according to which either one knows or does not know, something either is or is not:

> And, in each and all cases, it is possible for us either to know a thing or not to know it? I leave out of account for the moment becoming acquainted with things and forgetting, considered as falling between the two (*metaxú*). Our argument is not concerned with them just now. (*Theaet.* 188a)

This "guiding principle," as Heidegger calls it,[12] excludes, in a Parmenidean logic, the very possibility of *pseudès dóxa*, and of *dóxa* in general, as there is no opinion if there is no possibility of distinguishing a true discourse from a false one. The dimension of time—implicit in the possibility of remembering or forgetting, as the intermediary for knowing and not knowing—is thus essential to truth precisely because there would otherwise not be any way to distinguish it from falsehood. That there is such an intermediate dimension therefore involves placing Parmenides's ontology, for which something is or is not, under radical consideration. In this way, the distinction between possessing and having knowledge implicitly carries with it the ontological distinction between potential and actual. As Plato writes with the example of the pigeon coop still in mind, whoever possesses his birds by keeping them in an aviary at home has acquired "the power (*dynamis*) to take them and hold them whenever he wishes" (*Theaet.* 197c–d), a prelude to the definition of being itself as *dynamis* that Plato offers in the *Sophist.* What allows us to go "beyond" Parmenides is the very idea of a "beyond," the idea of a "more" in respect to being, or perhaps it would now be better to say, in respect to beings.

The "excess" of which the soul is capable in relation to sensation thus always appears as more of a peculiar capacity, or better, exactly as the "*possibility of,*" a *dynamis*: this is the ontological acquisition that allows Paremenideism to be overcome by introducing to it a principle of non-presentness, at the same time a lacking (what is not present *is* not) and an excess (even if it is not present, it can become so).

Plato introduces this capacity of the soul as an *analogical* capacity, able to place multiple things in relation and to identify their reciprocal relations:

> I think that these also are among the things the essence of which the soul most certainly views in their relations to one another, reflecting (*analogízetai*) within itself upon the past and present in relation to the future. (*Theaet.* 186a)

Heidegger comments on this passage by turning his attention to the fact that Plato grants the soul a capacity to place the various modes of time into relations, but above all to place the past and the present into relation with the future.[13] This particularity indicates the character of the soul as fundamentally open to the future, and thus dynamic and potential—its tendency toward something that still is not. The soul is in fact something that tends (*eporegétai*) toward Being, which is thus structurally different than the past and the present, namely, something essentially *not present* (the past being something that at least was present). In this definition of the soul, Heidegger thus sees a "fundamental connection between being and time," to the extent that "the relation to being is intrinsically a reckoning with time."[14]

The excess of Being is therefore principally futural. The *dynamis* installs a tension in the soul that carries it beyond what is given. This excess is not conceivable as a simple addition to the given; indeed, it is the condition of the very givenness of entities. As happens in Kant, the analogical, synthetic function does not follow from experience; it is rather its condition of possibility: only because experience *is already* synthesized, and that is thanks to time, is any analysis possible. And so Heidegger also writes:

> Thus, in the order of the inquiry, we can say that this excess is an addition to what is sensed. However, what we subsequently find here is in its nature and essence not "more" in the sense of addition (*Zugabe*), but on the contrary is the *pregiven* (*Vorgabe*).[15]

The a priori is thus configured not as a reality complete in itself, but as one that is incomplete, a *dynamis*, a possibility, and that is time.

The Ontological Background of *Alétheia*: Ontology of the Possible

The possibility of false discourse—and thus, correlatively, of true discourse—moves in sync with the possibility of time. The oblivion of time, in metaphysics, is in fact a forgetting of truth. For that reason even Nietzsche, in the moment in which he holds to a conception of truth as relative to what endures, is in Heidegger's view Platonic (of a Platonism that nevertheless is only a historiographical cliché).[16] Conversely, Heidegger's claim that the essence of truth is non-truth (*Un-Wahrheit*),[17] beyond its apparently contradictory formulation, expresses the idea that truth is not possible without a "background" from which it emerges, against which it is differentiated. The alpha privative of the word *alétheia* speaks to this "emerging," this self-constituting as a "more" in respect to the originary given. This mode of conceiving the truth can be considered a development of the phenomenological idea of truth as evidence—not the apodictic truth of Descartes, but the pure givenness of something to consciousness ("in the flesh"), which in this case is more precisely understood as pure emergence from a background that then recedes into non-presence. But this makes it so that the perception of a temporal difference differentiation cannot be disconnected from truth. The coming to be of what is manifested implicates a difference that is not in fact qualitative, a difference in content, but temporal, as a "before" and an "after." This is not at all a form of historicism, as it does not concern the temporality of the *contents* of truth, but the temporality of its form, of experience.

The connection between the discourse on truth and the discourse on *dóxa* is therefore understood on the basis of a necessity to introduce, in the gnoseological considerations of science, the ontological dimension of time. There is no truth without falsehood, which means that there is no truth without the possibility of the false, and thus of change, of "being able to not be." The challenge to Eleatism is taken up in the displacement of this negation: from "*not able* to be" (nonbeing is not) to "*able not* to be," which also expresses the passage from the ontology of presence and of necessity to the ontology of the possible and of the contingent.

This passage is what remains unthinkable for metaphysics and for science. The notorious Heideggerian expression "science does not think" has been subject to numerous misinterpretations, but I believe that its meaning ought to be understood against the background of this problematic. That science does not think means that it is always *positive*, that its thinking cannot proceed from anything but the positivity of entities, and that it aims for the perfect correspondence to this positivity; in contrast, philosophy shakes such positivity by introducing the possibility of negation, of nonbeing, the possibility that is carried to extreme radicality in the fundamentally metaphysical question "why are there beings at all rather than nothing?,"[18] a question that is rightly foreign to science. The very thought of *possibility* "splits" the positivity of the entity by opening it up to a dimension of possible negation. To think, for Heidegger, is to enter into this possibility of negation, that is, to negation as the possibility that "suspends" the real by turning it into something contingent.[19]

This sense of truth, one belonging to an ontology of the possible and the contingent, is for Heidegger guarded in the primordial experience of *alétheia*: it is the experience of the temporal difference between presence and absence, *Anwesenheit* and *Abwesenheit*, terms in which the meaning of the word *Wesen* resonates clearly.[20] In it, however, the simple positivity of *Wesen* is made dynamic by the prepositions *an-*(to go *to*) and *ab-*(to go away *from*). These prepositions introduce a temporal dimension that for Heidegger can also be expressed as truth and non-truth, *Wahrheit* and *Nicht-Wahrheit* respectively. This latter term, distinct from *Un-Wahrheit*,[21] which Heidegger reserves for being false as incorrectness, nonconformity or nonequivalence, is "What is *not yet* unhidden" or "what is *no longer* unhidden."[22] In the end, what Heidegger tries to express through the word *alétheia* and the recovery of the ontological dimension of possibility that it involves is the truly elementary experience—and, in this sense, *phenomenological* in a pre-philosophical way—of the fact that something changes, which appears and vanishes, the experience of passing, of day and night, of birth and death: the very experience of time.

The experience of truth is above all the experience of what exists, not in its immobile eternity, but in its mutability; it is the experience of time as the alternating of day and night, of presence and absence, of being and non-being. This primordial experience is that "revelation" that sustains philosophical research, the fundamental metaphysical question, "why is there something rather than nothing?" The experience of truth is the direct contact with the existent and with its possibility to no longer be. In the existential analysis it is made possible not through an intellectual inquiry, but through anxiety, the radical feeling that opens authentic understanding—that is, the understanding that every other truth cannot *not* be referred to this temporal background, or simply, what is temporal in a profound sense. A temporality that, to say it again, does not so much concern the content—which does not signify the arbitrary, relativistic variability of individual truths in function of time—but rather that concerns the *form* of truth (in the manner that for Kant time is the form of *all* phenomena in general, the very form of experience). The experience of truth—of ontological truth understood in this way—is therefore, for Heidegger, the experience of the form of experience, the *knowledge* of its temporality.

This is not merely subjective, but has the same objectivity of every historical phenomenon. And in the same way that *alétheia* is not subjective, so too is its opposite, the concealing and "forgetting" (*léthe*):

> It is typical of the Greek language to say *léthe* (being hidden in the sense of being-gone) of the *beings* to which man should be able to comport himself. The Greeks say that beings are gone, so that one knows nothing more of them. We say, by contrast, that someone who no longer knows anything is "somewhere else," "not all there." It is therefore quite wrong to translate *léthe* as forgetting in the ordinary sense of a subjective psychological event.[23]

The true sense of the Heideggerian conception of truth is therefore not at all one of its subjectification.[24] Forgetting and concealing are not "psychological" functions, but ontological modalities of the entity. *Alétheia* is their movement, as the passage from one to the other, from absence to presence. Far from being a sort of subjectification, it is instead the attempt to restore truth to its purer ontological dimension, which is not the realm of eternal being—which is only the result of a metaphysical abstraction—but of time and of history, that is, of physics. "Objective" is the happening in which we are always coinvolved. The "forgetting" is in the first place, and that is objectively, the fleeing and going-away of the entity, and subjectively, the attitude that eliminates this going-away in order to affix itself to presence. Metaphysics is born from this *subjective* forgetting.

It is clear that the "overcoming" of such a forgetting, or even the reconsideration of the question of truth in terms of *alétheia,* also carries with it the overcoming of the metaphysical conception of truth. That means, moreover, that one can no longer speak of truth if not in terms of history. Plato's recourse to a myth, that of the cave, is due to the fact that a narrative, used to expound his "theory" of truth, is not for Heidegger simply a didactic fact, but a demand inscribed in the very concept of truth, as it happens, as it comes to being. Only as history and beginning with history is it possible to grasp the profound meaning—the *essence*—of truth.

The idea that the experience of truth is *fundamentally* the very experience of time, in its not at all subjective, but more radically objective, dimension—an objectivity that no subject could ever dominate, because by its essence it evades the repeatability of the scientific method—constitutes the profound nucleus of the hermeneutic conception of truth that leads Gadamer to the revaluation of the truth content of the human sciences (cf. *infra*, chapter 5).

Chapter 4

Truth and Transformation

Truth Changes

That the *experience* of truth is also the experience of time entails a very particular conception of the role that the predicate "true" has in our speech. First of all, it is not a redundant element, and thus a superfetation or pleonasm, because it adds something to the judged content of the judgment.[1] Such a notion of truth was already under scrutiny by William James: it would suppose that reality is stable and complete, ready for all eternity, and that the agreement between it and our ideas is their unique and unanalyzable virtue.

> As that intrinsic excellence, their truth has nothing to do with our experiences. It adds nothing to the content of experience. It makes no difference to reality itself; it is supervenient, inert, static, a reflection merely.[2]

The insistence on the logical superfluity of the predicate "true," and therefore on its uselessness, completely leaves aside the *experiential* moment that is connected to it, the fact that by its means we recognize or confirm that something in our experience is changed, *and thus has produced a difference.*

By introducing the vertical sign into his ideography in order to distinguish the act of judgment from the mere content of assertions, Frege was clearly aware of the need to give expression to this difference.[3] It is the difference that exists between "I smell the scent of violets" and "It is true that I smell the scent of violets." These assertions have exactly the same content, such that it seems that nothing has been added to thought through the attribution of the property of truth. It nonetheless records a *meaningful* event, the fact that "the scientist after much hesitation and laborious researches can finally say 'my conjecture is true.' The meaning of the word 'true,'" Frege then concludes, "seems to be altogether sui generis."[4]

Frege very clearly expresses the idea that the redundant character of "true"—*in terms of its content*—does not diminish, but in fact makes even more cogent, its *experientially* non-indifferent character. Perhaps the hermeneutic protest against the conception of truth as correspondence, which would turn it into a transparent glass without any distortions between the thing and its representation, between reality and its reflection—to the point of negating itself—is nothing more than the protest against its presumed uselessness: a protest that, incidentally, goes hand in hand with the objection turned against the uselessness of Being, against its reduction to mere *flatus vocis*, or against the superfluousness of the copula in judgment. From the point of view of hermeneutics and a hermeneutic theory of truth, what should be recovered is the experiential dimension that "true" undeniably expresses, and whose meaning is the transformative effect that it records and of which it is the trace. After Nietzsche—a name by which we designate the radical awareness of the logical uselessness of the predicate "true" and of its total overturning in the practical realm, as Vattimo demonstrated by discussing the doctrine of the eternal return[5]—the concept of truth has lost none of its appeal for us; and yet, perhaps it has acquired another one, no longer relative to the question "what is truth?" but to the question "what does truth *make*?"

The Pragmatization of Hermeneutics

This pragmatic tendency in the conception of truth is particularly evident in Richard Rorty, who not only undertook a pragmatization of analytic philosophy, but a corresponding "pragmatization of hermeneutics." For Rorty, pragmatism consists in the attempt to get rid of Truth (with the big *T*) and replace it with truth (with the small *t*)—that is, get rid of the ideal that has characterized the literary genre invented by Plato known as Philosophy (with a big *P*), which Platonists and positivists share in common, and replace it with philosophy (with a small *p*). With this Truth set aside, what remains is truth, which has nothing to do with absolute Reality, but with circumstances, situations, in which a given claim is shown to be useful or efficacious relative to certain goals: "true" is what gives rise to practical results deemed acceptable relative to definite needs or interests, or that is useful in a definite context for definite goals.[6]

In the defense of the pragmatic notion of truth, Rorty sees a radicalization of the Baconian idea of science, cleansed of its metaphysical—and even epistemological—concretions still present in positivism. The pragmatist

> shares with the positivist the Baconian and Hobbesian notion that knowledge is power, a tool for coping with reality. But he carries this Baconian point through to its extreme, as the positivist does not. He drops the notion of truth as correspondence with reality altogether, and says that modern science does not enable us to cope because it corresponds, it just plain enables us to cope.[7]

Rorty therefore lets all that is not verifiable in pragmatic, or even *behavioral*, terms fall under the test of an unavoidable "Ockham's Razor": that is, a test for every element that could take on some cognitive valence. One gets to pragmatism through Berkeley, who without mincing words, argued for the uselessness of the word "Being";[8] however, more radically than for Berkeley, even words like "idea" and "mind"[9] lack any pragmatic utility, and thus any meaning, for Rorty. To use an expression from Wittgenstein, they are like those "wheels turning idly" that we would be better off without.[10] According to Rorty, this Wittgensteinian idea nicely expresses the pragmatical "verificationist" intuition according to which "every difference must *make* a difference."[11]

I think that this idea is shared: truth produces differences, that is, transformations. The question that still seems debatable is the role that these differences assume, from the point of view of Rorty, and a pragmatic one in general, as they serve to *verify* a certain hypothesis or certain change—not a change in ideas, but literally a change in *vocabulary*. In fact, from the moment that we are always and only dealing with behaviors or practices lacking cognitive value, the overcoming of metaphysics could be promised by a simple change in vocabulary, namely, a change in uses of speech. It is like saying that it is sufficient to produce a certain transformation in behavior—in the use of certain words rather than others—in order to produce new truths and new experiences. A new vocabulary does not *express* a new experience—from that moment there is no longer anything to express, not even a new understanding of Being—but, above all, produces it. And if it produces it, it is by that very act *verified*, and therefore better than an old one that keeps things the way they are. According to William James's definition, who was still speaking dangerously of "ideas," "*True ideas are those that we can assimilate, validate, corroborate and verify. False ideas are those that we cannot.*"[12]

The Hermeneuticization of Pragmatism

This verificationist attitude seems to be the most controversial and debatable aspect of Rortyan pragmatism, the one most incompatible with the hermeneutic conception of truth. Paradoxically, Rorty parts from the idea of the redundant character of truth, and of the many other linguistic elements clearly useless from the point of view of a theory of truth based on representation and correspondence (as being, idea, or mind), in order to erase any right they have in a pragmatistic theory of truth. On the contrary, the hermeneutic condemnation of the theory of truth as reflection, far from confirming the redundant and useless character of such elements, brings about its revaluation in *experiential* terms.

The pragmatistic verificationism of Rorty consists in the reciprocal implication of truth and effectuality, because there is no *pragmatic* difference between "it works because it's true" and "it's true because it works," any more than between "it's pious because the gods love it" and "the gods love it because it's pious."[13] If there were a difference, this would be a difference that has no effect. The intuitive realist instead claims exactly this sort of thing, namely, "that some differences can be real *without* making a difference," or that sometimes the *ordo essendi* is different from the *ordo cognoscendi*.[14]

Through an inversion of the realist disarticulation of the pragmatic-verificationistic equivalence between truth and effectuality, hermet neutics takes into consideration the possibility of *a difference that makes a difference without being real*, which corresponds to nothing representational—the possibility I would employ as the principle of a hermeneuticization of pragmatism. This shows the incompatibility between hermeneutics and pragmatism, at least in the Rortyan version. That some differences can be produced without anything *real* corresponding to them is the very principle of experience. The Heideggerian notion of ontological difference works in this very way: it thematizes a difference—the one between Being and entities—that does not correspond to any object in the world.

The ontological difference is a phenomenon of understanding, or more precisely, the understanding of a difference: it expresses the possibility of understanding the real as something that can be different from what it is now, that is, as a possibility. Far from prioritizing the present or the real, the ontological difference tends rather to show continuously the "difference," the gap, between being and truth, or in other words, to *falsify* it: it *makes difference* in the sense that it agrees to understand reality as transformable. By falsifying reality, it disarticulates the pragmatist equivalence between truth and effectuality by showing negatively the possibility of a diverse world. Here one finds, moreover, the critical *chance* of hermeneutics: to hold open this gap, to conceive of truth itself as always open, and not as completion or actuality. It is the "experience of time," because it poses a difference between a before and an after, between that which we believed was true and that which now is shown to be true, between the past and the present, and between the present and the future. By showing this temporality of the real, the experience of truth allows reality itself to be understood as a possibility: the opening is turned intrinsically toward the future and toward new possibilities.

The function of the ontological difference—and thus of the relation and of the gap existing between the understanding of Being and the constitution of entities, the possibility of sense and the actuality of meaning, hypothesis, and proof, truth as opening and truth as equivalence[15]—seems for this reason to be completely analogous to the function of the *modus tollens* in Popper's critique of verificationism (and of its criterion of meaning).[16] The understanding that the entity *is not* Being makes it so that the truth of Being is never resolved and never completely coincides with the truth of the entity. Thus, if even from the hermeneutic point of view truth is granted an effectual power (the truth changes), it does not follow that the inverse is valid, namely, that effectuality could be considered the sufficient reason of truth. The institution of an equivalence between truth and effectuality, typically of the verificationist sort, is nothing other than another form of Parmenideanism—that is, of monism (whether idealistic or materialistic, as in the very case of Rorty)—as a result of the attempt to institute an equivalence between Being and thinking, between the *ordo essendi* and the *ordo cognoscendi*. At least since Heidegger, hermeneutics reacts *against* this form of positivism, not surprisingly by once again taking up in grand style reasons typical of Aristotelian ontology, such as the multiplicity of modes of Being and the concept of "possibility."

The ontological difference is not a *real* difference, because it does not constitute a predicative difference that would distinguish between two diverse objects; it is not a difference between two res. As not real, in the sense of *Realität*, it is nevertheless effectual, *wirklich*: it makes difference, produces a transformation, in the way that Heidegger, in his 1921 course dedicated to the *Phenomenology of Religious Life*, speaks of Christian *conversion*: "something remains unchanged, and yet it is radically changed [*etwas bleibt unverändert, und doch wird es radikal geändert*]."[17]

The Truth of Experience: The Myth of the Cave

The transformational conception of truth that is constitutive of hermeneutic experience is expressed by Vattimo, in the introduction to his Italian translation of *Truth and Method*, with the idea that true experience (*esperienza vera*) is the *true* experience (*vera esperienza*), namely, "what effectively modifies whoever experiences it."[18] This difference in the placement of "true" aims to clarify the sense (of the understanding) of the ontological difference.[19] *True* experience is in fact "what effectively modifies whoever experiences it;" it is the bearer of a different *understanding*, such that it modifies him and his entire world, and that in no way consists in the predicative modification of the subject or of the object, if we want to say it this way, but of their relation, in the manner that Hegel uses to illustrate the process of phenomenological experience. *True* experience is not what confirms true experience, but is in fact what falsifies it: by negating its definiteness, it opens new possibilities. It is experience free for further experiences and further transformations.

The connection between *true* experience and the understanding of ontological difference consists in the fact that the falsification of true experience carries with it the understanding of its modifiability, of its being able to be something other than how it is, what is precisely the profound content of the notion of "ontological difference." *True* experience in fact has the constitution of negation, of "not this way, but otherwise," or even of falsification.

In this way the ontological difference allows truth to be conceived as opening and to define its temporality—in conformity with the ontology of the possible that we have seen emerge from the discussion about *alethès dóxa* in Plato—as future, by granting it one of the typical traits of the pragmatic conception of truth: in contrast with classical empiricism, which measured the truth of an idea in respect to the past, that is, in respect of experience already transpired, from a pragmatic point of view truth is instead principally directed toward the future, in function of its effects.[20] But there would be no future if experience itself were not first and foremost understood as transformable. The ontological difference allows this opening of experience onto the future: it is really, we can say in Kantian terms—and even more of the Kantian a priori, which defines a realm immutable in itself, the immutable in the mutable—the "form of *possible* experience."

The transformational conception of truth appears at first glance decisively anti-Platonic, and above all, Rortyan pragmatism is directed against Platonism (not so much against positivism, with which it instead maintains good neighborly relations):[21] with the name "Platonism" we mean in fact a conception for which the true world is an intangible world, neither changed nor touched, not even marginally, by experience. This idea seems to me a true prejudice, even in light of the reading that Heidegger gives of the myth of the cave in *Plato's Doctrine of Truth*, because it misrecognizes the connection, strong and indissoluble, that Plato instills between knowledge and ethics, theory and praxis. Since the beginning of Book VII of the *Republic*, as Heidegger does not fail to emphasize, the problem that Plato poses is that of education (*paideía*) and of the lack of education, that is, of *Bildung*. The process of knowledge is configured then soon after as a process of self-transformation.

The myth of the cave in the end seems to describe in a rather effective way what I called the "transformational dimension of truth." The myth in fact presents a series of transformations, of conversions of the glance, dramatized in successive events that unfold in different locations. Heidegger writes that *paideía* is "leading the whole human being in the turning around of his or her essence,"[22] that is, a transformation of *sense*: a "turning around of their gazes as a disruption of customary behavior and of current opinion."[23] By describing scenes and different objects (shadows, statues, reflections, ideas), even entities with predicative, *real*, differences, Plato tries to express the change within the process of knowing, which is a change both of the knowing subject and of the known object: a change that is at the same time a process of ethical elevation, even of progressive liberation, the result of *modal* differences. One knows more, one ascends to ever higher levels of truth, to the degree that one is freer, and one becomes more free the more one knows.

The so-called Platonic dualism between the world of ideas and the world of experience (repeated countless times and in countless ways in the history of philosophy), which is the metaphysical cornerstone of the equivalence theory of truth, is dissolved in the "transformational conception of truth." It does not regard the passage from a pre-experiential state (mental, logical, conceptual, cognitive) to an experiential one, but alludes to a transformation within experience: "true" expresses a transmutation of experience, the transmutation that Plato describes—but how to do it otherwise?—by going back to diverse places, objects, and forms in order to express ultimately only diverse conditions and modes of experience. By making the Platonic dialectic dynamic, Hegel had knowingly interpreted the myth of the cave in procedural terms. Every progress in knowing carries with it a transformation of the object and of the subject of knowing. Knowledge, in short, is not external to reality, but is a constitutive part of it. Truth is the motor of reality, which, by virtue of knowledge, grows, increases, transforms, to the point that a prior state recognized as no longer true passes away into another and takes on another form.

I dare say that there is also a pragmatic dimension to the Platonic conception of truth: truth changes, changes the subject and the object, produces differences represented as diverse worlds, transforms and opens onto new experiences. And all of them are true experiences. It is noteworthy in fact that the word "false" never appears in the Platonic narration of the myth of the cave; there are only incremental levels of truth, expressed as Heidegger notes, through the use of the comparative (*alethésteron*) and the superlative (*alethéstaton*) of the adjective *alethés*. This truth is the experience of phenomenological truth, according to which "what is" is for that reason true, in the terms in which it is given.

Nevertheless, the content of myth is not totally resolved in the illustration of these true experiences. There is something more, which is revealed as parallel to the ascent toward ever-truer worlds, to ever-greater levels of reality, and that is what I would call the process of *true* experience, which becomes such only at the end; at the beginning it is a *false experience*. The Platonic myth of the cave begins exactly with a condition of false experience: it is constituted by the condition of enslavement of those individuals stuck in the cave, a condition of confinement and lack of freedom.[24] An experience that is not free is not a *true* experience; it becomes more true only if it is the product and the cause of an increase in freedom. It is not clear in the myth if this possibility of the *true* experience—of open experience, unrestricted, free—is a presupposition or a consequence of true experience. Perhaps both things are true, but there is no doubt, however, that the slave's possibility of accessing new experiences is bound to the possibility of being freed from his initial condition, in which he is restricted to looking only in front of himself, without any possibility of movement.

How this initial liberation arrives is exactly what Plato fails to explain. One can suppose that the awareness transmitted by the philosopher reawakens in the slave the possibility of another world, and thus his thirst for freedom; but how this might have happened to the philosopher is referred back to the ancestral memory of a primordial truth, to the anamnesis of the world of ideas, of a *different* world, that is, to the memory of a difference, a *chorismós*—what Heidegger expressed as the memory of the difference between Being and entities, the ontological difference.[25] This memory is what casts a shadow of *falsity* on the true world, to show it as less true than what it seems. In short, it begins to appear as falsifiable, as liable to being seen in a different light or in another way, that is, as transmutable. Truth therefore transforms on the condition of being, above all, the condition of the falsification of the world that is before us, of the *present* world. It is as if to say that the *true* experience begins as the falsification of true experience. The more that false experience becomes true, the more the world, first understood to be true, becomes false.

What makes the Platonic doctrine of truth something more than a simplistically pragmatic one is the dimension of *true* experience, that is, its coupling of the problem of education with *paideía* rather than with mere behavior: it is a global "revolution," which concerns the removal of the entire human being

> from the region where they first encounter things and transferring and accustoming them to another realm where beings appear. This transfer is possible only by the fact that everything that has been heretofore manifest to human beings, as well as the way in which it has been manifest, gets transformed. Whatever has been unhidden to human beings at any given time, as well as the manner of its unhiddenness, has to be transformed.[26]

This unhiddenness is truth. The aim of this process is freedom; its presupposition is the understanding of possible difference between Being and entities, a difference that is *not real* but capable of producing effects. It does not have any descriptive value in respect to actual experience, but only in respect to a possible experience, an experience that is *free* for further experiences.

The "Anticonformist" Character of Truth

Plato tried to thematize the unbreakable connection between truth and freedom as the constitutive connection of *Bildung*. Its reference to what we have called "*true* experience" is probably a protest against the pragmatical behavior of the sophists, for whom truth is reduced once and for all to the incomparable power of language, able on its own to produce admirable effects. Hermeneutics for Rorty is ultimately reduced to this, and the edification for which it advocates appears completely unchained from every truth; it is an inventive, creative, even self-creative act. Edification is a here meneutic activity that consists in finding new, better, and more interesting ways of speaking so that we are able to reconceive ourselves and thus help us to become "new beings,"[27] "happier, freer and more flexible,"[28] through the adoption of new vocabularies. As Watson, champion of behaviorism, said, by influencing behavior it is possible to train for anything. Edification thus appears as a purely *behavioral* rather than an *experiential* fact, to the point of assuming a particularly manipulative character.

In this view, hermeneutics is "abnormal science"—*revolutionary*, to use an expression from Thomas Kuhn—but in a merely aesthetic sense because it invents new languages and thus is able to bring about new behaviors. But this is certainly not the direction in which the Gadamerian defense of the truth-bearing character of the human sciences, and of art in particular, was going; rather, it was responding to the same demand of the scientific revolutions which, according to Kuhn, are not born arbitrarily, but due to *internal* ruptures in the science, that is, in the moment when a demand for truth *exceeds*, in a manner of speaking, the being-true of the prevailing paradigm.

This experience of rupture, which requires a different articulation of sense, is what we have defined as "hermeneutic falsificationism," and for which is central the experience of nonfulfillment, of the interruption of the reference described by Heidegger in *Being and Time*: when something *no longer functions* I am immediately aware that it *is* other than what it was, and that therefore in general the being of the entity is not the same as the entity. What role does "nonfunctioning"—or in pragmatic terms, falsity—play in Rorty? For him—as affirmed in a debate with Umberto Eco—to use a screwdriver to scratch one's ears,[29] despite its evident misuse, would indicate a new invention, like the introduction of a new word in an old lexicon. For Heidegger, on the other hand, this is exactly the type of phenomenon in which the ontological difference stands forth. Such an interruption of functionality is an *event*, something that, far from depending on subjective will (Rorty would say "on *private* being"), places subjectivism itself under consideration when it acquires an *objective* dimension, in the sense of it being independent from me. Such an event is "revolutionary," in the sense that it requires a conversion of one's glance that includes oneself and the world, what Kuhn would call a paradigm shift, which not only redefines one's self in a manner not solely private, but also redefines the world in which one exists.

The emphasis on the romantic element in the Rortyan conception of hermeneutics makes it so that interpretation is configured as a totally creative act that soars over one's head and cancels itself out, as with Kant's example of the dove that would like to fly without the friction of the air. On the contrary, even in romantic hermeneutics, interpretation is an act that attempts to recompose the sense of the text, to continue its *discourse*, beginning from that experience of an interruption of sense. In doing this, hermeneutics has truly conceived its task as a continual process of universalization, of the fusion of horizons, of the extension of the "we," thanks to the dialogical procedure that in itself wants to be a nonsubjective process. In it, as Gadamer says, lies the very logic of dialogue, that of question and answer, in which one co-responds to something that is sent from someone other than we, from the other, and that guides the interlocutors, and not the other way around. In such a way Gadamerian hermeneutics is clearly directed toward the constitution of a historical substantiality that is condensed in the concept of the "classic."

In the rhetorical strategy of the pragmatist it is nevertheless possible to rediscover something functionally analogous to the notion of ontological difference: it is the effect, more or less intentional, that his argument produces, namely, that of "changing the subject."[30] Faced by a problem that is boring or lacking a pragmatic solution, the pragmatist changes the subject. The eminently revolutionary character of such a gesture needs to be recognized. By avoiding the argument, avoiding the game one was supposed to play, the pragmatist enacts a rupture, an interruption, gives rise to a non sequitur, to an anacoluthon, analogous to falsification for Gadamer or the broken tool for Heidegger. But this gesture would be completely fruitless, and thus be merely irritating, if it were to remain solely on a behavioral plane. It is without doubt that its efficacy depends on a different *understanding*—or, if one prefers, on the understanding of a difference—which can provoke the interlocutor, showing him another possibility, that of being able to "change the subject." Without this effect of understanding, nothing revolutionary would ever be able to be invented.

The revolutionary effect of hermeneutics *above all* appeals to the possibility of a different understanding, expressed in the notion of the "ontological difference." The human sciences are ultimately not concerned with another, different truth, or even with no truth at all, but rather with the diversifying *effects* of truth, or with truth as the possibility of being diverted. One can even say that, especially since Gadamer, the defense of the truth-bearing character of the human sciences was nothing other than the attempt to recover the experientially nonredundant, and thus transformative, dimension of truth.[31] A notion of truth that is *also* present in the natural sciences despite their artificial demarcation: what is "human" in the natural sciences is precisely their undeniable contribution to the transformative process of humanity, that is, to its *Bildung*. What such a non-verificationist concept of truth shows to understanding —based on an effect that is falsifying, *anti-conformist*, and productive of ontological difference—is the essential modifiability of reality: the idea that, as Vattimo writes, "a different world is possible."[32]

Chapter 5

More Than the Real

The Extra-Methodicalness of Truth as the Objectivity of Happening

The hermeneutic experience of truth is not something subjective: both the Heideggerian insistence on *alétheia*, as the experience of coming to being, and also the Gadamerian insistence on falsification carry with them a reorganization and a decentering of the subject. And, as much as it seems paradoxical, the coherent result of this conception of truth is precisely the defense of its extra-methodical character that Gadamer undertakes in *Truth and Method.*

One of the more serious misunderstandings of Gadamer's *Truth and Method* is in fact to interpret its title as a pair of alternatives or as an opposition: truth or method—or even worse, as a dissociation, both from the truth and from the method, because of their complicity in the modern scientific revolution, such that the reasons for rejecting the latter would also lead one to reject the former. The consequence of this misunderstanding is the idea that hermeneutics either has nothing to do with truth or defends a concept of truth essentially and completely incompatible with methodicalness.

Yet it is clear, especially regarding the first of these consequences, that Gadamer, far from denying the truthfulness of the experiences definable as hermeneutical (notably art and history), makes a great effort in *Truth and Method* to defend their capacity to bear truth. The target of his criticism is rather the alleged exclusivity of methodical truth, reliant upon experimental verification, and the consequent idea that rationality itself coincides with the methodological and ontological requirements of scientific experimentation (repeatability, and therefore the possible idealization, of the phenomenon.) In reality, the method lets experience be available to repetition, through a process of idealization, for a subject that in this way is able to control and dominate it. "In prescinding from the primarily experienceable and familiar totality of our world, it has been developed into a knowledge of manipulable relationship by means of isolating experimentation."[1]

The reference to the concept of play as leitmotiv for an ontology of the work of art is Gadamer's claim on a dimension of experience that escapes such methodical controllability. In play, the subject experiments with the impossibility of being the master of reality, of being able to control it completely. The technical mastery of nature requires it to be bound within the conditions of the possibility of method, which are technical conditions that depend on their human realizability. Modern science, as Kant writes in the preface to the second edition of the *Critique of Pure Reason*, has found its sure path in the experimental method, through which reason learned not to allow itself to be kept, as it were, in nature's leading strings, but to constrain nature "to give answer to questions of reason's own determining."[2] The experiment—which, as Apel writes, "translates the interrogation of the human into the language of nature"[3]—is nothing but the constitution of a controllable realm where it is not nature that imposes its course, but rather the human who imposes its sovereignty on nature.

In this way, far from being the extreme expression of the objectivity of science, the reduction of experience to methodical testability appears as the surreptitious expression of its subjectification, by making experience available to a subject that in this way becomes able to dominate it. *Truth and Method* is entirely crisscrossed by a polemic against modern subjectivism. Its criticism against the reduction of truth to the conditions of the method is not therefore an anti-objectivistic dispute; on the contrary, it is a dispute against the subjectivism that stands at the heart of methodical rationality. Or, in other words, it is the elaboration of a different concept of objectivity that consists no longer in the systematic connection between phenomena—experimentally reproducible, through their idealization—, but rather in the happening of something that, although not methodically repeatable and verifiable, is nonetheless laden with effectuality. It is quite obvious that historical truth is precisely so. One cannot repeat the French Revolution, and indeed it is impossible to repeat any historical event just as it has happened; nevertheless, it "is true" in the sense that it has produced some effects, and its very comprehension goes on producing effects.

The basic thesis of *Truth and Method* is therefore more clearly explained by its original title, which according to Gadamer was changed at the publisher's request: *Geschehen und Verstehen*, that is, "happening and understanding." Unlike the pair "truth and method," "happening and understanding" suggests no opposition: it is clearly a correlation between an ontological phenomenon (the happening) and a consequent cognitive modality (the understanding). In light of this correlation, the defense of an extra-methodical experience of truth can be understood then as a defense of an objectivity much more radical than that of science—the objectivity of what happens, of what surprises us like a ball unexpectedly thrown at us that we have to catch and, perhaps, throw again (as in the image from Rilke's poem that opens *Truth and Method*). This friendly and not overpowering modality encountered in the event is the modality that philosophical hermeneutics opposes to technical mastery. It is what Heidegger called "openness" (*Erschlossenheit*): the idea that truth is above all what, *subjectively*, demands our openness, our capability of receiving it, of co-responding to it, and, *objectively*, what "opens" the experience, showing us something new that was not there before and that goes beyond our expectations.[4] This happening is an event in the sense of an "accidentality" that is and remains as such: accidental, within the experience, even when redeemed or overcome in a second-degree reflection that inscribes it within a superior order, in a rational or physical consequentiality (which is the function of understanding). We can nonetheless ask whether such an experiential accidentality does not refer, and in which sense it does refer, to a more radical, *ontological* accidentality. In my opinion, the philosophical perspective from which Heidegger in particular works, above all his considerations on being as *Ereignis* and on the fundamental metaphysical question ("why are there beings at all instead of nothing?") goes exactly in this direction: thinking a fundamental accidentality of the real, not so much in the sense that whatever happens is accidental, but in the sense that reality as a whole is something contingent—that it is there but could not be there. In this way, the whole of reality is by Heidegger "suspended" to the accidental, inverting the Aristotelian axiom according to which the substance (what persists) precedes the accident (what passes, happens, and disappears).[5]

In conclusion, the reference to the concept of play in Gadamerian ontology has the aim to thematize an activity, which like experimentation presents various distinguishing marks that we can synthesize in the following manner:

1. Play is not a methodical activity, but always preserves a ludic aspect: Gadamer's preferred example is not in fact one marked by games with strict rules such as chess—which is the example that appears most frequently in Wittgenstein—but activities such as playing with a ball. This means that for Gadamer play

is above all *enérgeia*, activity. It is, to use a distinction that exists in English, but not in Italian, *play* rather than a *game*—the game as it is played and not as an ensemble of rules;[6]

2. Play is an intersubjective activity, which in principle also involves others (another player or a spectator): this intersubjective dimension is the way Gadamer protects it from the subjectivistic reductions of modern aesthetics. In fact, as it is not the function of a subject who dominates it, play instead presents a dimension of "objectivity" superior even to the objectivity of sciences, because it eludes the subject's control and is therefore quite independent of it. The extra-methodical truth is experienced *outside* of subjective control and is thus unique, unrepeatable (and therefore not ultimately verifiable), an event which is however no less objective. The notion itself of "objectivity" is here transformed: it is no longer the *systemic* objectivity of a natural phenomenon that can be traced back to laws, but rather the objectivity of what happens, the *historical* objectivity that we also meet in natural occurrences (every natural event, although referable to laws, *makes* history, is namely a particular event), and, above all, in human action;

3. Play is repetition, but even though it is always the *same* game, it is also always different, because it is subject to accidents that cannot be completely controlled: this "room for play," which makes it to some extent unforeseeable, is essential to its nature, which is presented as the inextricable weaving of regulation and flexibility, necessity and accidentality, domination and freedom. At this point, the question thus concerns, on the one hand, the nature of this repetition, and on the other hand, the nature of truth that is tried out within it.

The Abstraction of the Experimental Consciousness and the Temporality of Presentation

The particular form of repetition at stake in the concept of play corresponds to a diverse temporality, "difficult to grasp on the basis of the usual experience of temporal succession."[7] It is not one of sequentiality, of the succession of one present to another. Here Gadamer clearly introduces a distinction between diverse forms of temporality similar to that theorized by Heidegger in *Being and Time* as the distinction between authentic temporality and inauthentic temporality. The inauthentic temporality of sequentiality is that of the aesthetic consciousness, which, in the same manner that it undertakes the abstracting subjectivity of scientific experimentation in respect to a natural phenomenon, also considers the work of art as abstracted from its world, lacking in essential ontological references:

> What we call a work of art and experience aesthetically depends on a process of abstraction. By disregarding everything in which a work is rooted (its original context of life, and the religious or secular function that give it significance), it becomes visible as the "pure work of art." In performing this abstraction, aesthetic consciousness performs a task that is positive in itself. It shows what a pure work of art is, and allows it to exist in its own right. I call this "aesthetic differentiation."[8]

Aesthetic differentiation consists in presenting the work by leaving aside all of those extra-aesthetic elements such as purpose, intention, meanings, and contents, that place it into its world and that contribute in a definite way to defining the fullness of its meaning, in order to retain the one "aesthetic quality." In this way, it shows an "unlimited sovereignty over everything,"[9] similar to that of experimental consciousness. There is in fact a correspondence between the abstracting attitude, which leads to the formation of scientific experiment (i.e., the methodical-experimental consciousness), and the attitude of aesthetic consciousness, which operates an analogous reduction of the work of art to its pure ahistorical essentiality. This parallelism is also evident in the particular temporality of the scientific consciousness, on the one hand, and the temporality of the aesthetic consciousness, on the other. Actually, both reduce the phenomenon under consideration to its pure punctuality, an *Erlebnis* completely cut off from other experiences; thus, both conceive time as a chronological succession of such *Erlebnisse*, namely, of instants isolated and reduced to their normative and aesthetic abstraction. The surreptitious subjectivism of the scientific consciousness and the more explicit one of the aesthetic consciousness are thus shown in their particular temporality.[10]

The result of this abstracting operation performed by the aesthetic consciousness on the work of art is the institution of the museum. The museum can actually be considered the laboratory of the aesthetic consciousness: the place where the artistic phenomenon can be reduced to its pure ideality, decontextualized, and organized according to mere chronological succession.

To this inauthentic temporality Gadamer opposes an "authentic" temporality, that of presentation (*Darstellung*), typical of the works of art that cannot exist unless they are presented (musical, theatrical, literary works). It involves the impossibility of splitting the phenomenon under consideration from its temporal concreteness, which implies a particular consubstantiality between the original and its repetition, to such an extent that the work itself could not exist without its re-presentation.[11] Such a temporality also concerns play, as activity, *enérgeia*, and those events that mark social life, such as festivals, celebrations, and anniversaries. The festival, for instance, exists only as it is celebrated. With each recurrence, such events are still identified as "the same event"—not on the basis of their factual identity (no festival is really identical to another one, previous or future), but on the basis of their re-actualization of an originary event. It remains present in them, and acquires meaning thanks precisely to its repeated presentation:

> For the essence of the festival, its historical connections are secondary. As a festival it is not an identity like a historical event, but neither is it determined by its origin so that there was once the "real" festival—as distinct from the way in which it later came to be celebrated. From its inception—whether instituted in a single act or introduced gradually—the nature of a festival is to be celebrated regularly. Thus its own original essence is always to be something different (even when celebrated in exactly the same way). An entity that exists only by always being something different is temporal in a more radical sense than everything that belongs to history. It has its being only in becoming and return.[12]

The festival and its rituality are then Gadamer's answer to the idealizing repeatability—and thus abstraction—of the experimental method: while the experimental consciousness abstracts from the differences, including temporal ones, in order to attain the essentiality of the phenomenon in its ahistorical identity—as a mere expression of a physical law, since the historical reality of the experiment is quite inessential to this aim—the essential eventuality of the phenomenon emerges in the rite, without which the original itself would have no significance. In a word, what appears as inessential in the experiment—the historical fact of its presentation—is instead essential in the rite. It is not yet clear, however, what the ontological relevance of this repetition might be.

It can seem, first of all, that this conception of the essential temporality of historical experience, of which the aesthetic one is a particular case, is suitable only to the works of the transient arts, such as music, theatre, or literature, which do not exist unless they are presented. But Gadamer holds that it is possible to see the spatial equivalent of such a temporality in the concept of the *picture*. Like the presentation, the picture is not a mere repetition, that is, a simple copy. A play or a festival is not, so to say, a simple remake of a past event but is its re-actualization and is itself an event; it is because of this re-actualization that the event it repeats reconfirms its primacy as *event*. In the same way, the picture does not simply reflect a certain reality, but is the self-presentation of a certain reality in a different intensity of its being: "The world that appears in the play of presentation (*Darstellung*) does not stand like a copy to the real world, but is that world in the heightened truth of its being."[13] The presentation, or the picture, therefore presents the real in an intensive increase of its being. The concept of mimesis, therefore, does not point to a copy, but rather to the "appearance of what is presented."[14]

It can seem as if the eminent form of the picture is the reflected image. But, while it cannot exist without its original,[15] the opposite happens in the case of the aesthetic picture, where the original cannot exist without the picture. If there were no presentative re-actualization, there would be no original:

> Hence presentation remains essentially tied to the original represented in it. But it is more than a copy. That the representation is a picture—and not the original itself—does not mean anything negative, any mere diminution of being, but rather an autonomous reality. So the relation of the picture to the original is basically quite different than in the case of a copy. *It is no longer a one-sided relationship*. That the picture has its own reality means the reverse for what is pictured, namely that it comes to presentation in the representation. It presents itself there.[16]

This characterization of the picture—according to which it is not a copy and not even a mere reflection—is helpful for understanding the conception of truth that here is in sight. The picture—as reproduction or perfect copy—and the mirror are actually the most common metaphors for truth: a very powerful metaphor, which had, and still has, great success[17] and was already the object of criticism by William James who, when contesting the "indifferent" character of truth, was also contesting, as we have seen, the idea that it could be conceived as a "pure reflection." The significance of this metaphor is found in the "transparent" character of the mind, which is all the more capable of reflecting reality correctly, without distortions, the more it is transparent. This self-suppression of the mind is the sign of the absolute objectivity of knowledge. But Gadamer considers this paradoxical self-suppression of the mind to be the greatest deception,[18] as it is not possible to consider the real independently of the knowledge one has of it. We then need a new, different way to conceive the relation between reality, copy, reflection, and picture. In particular, the ontological peculiarity of the picture is neither a simple addition (like a copy) nor suppression (like the reflection), but rather something "more": "This kind of picture is not a copy, for it represents something which, without it, would not present itself in this way. It says something about the original [e.g., a good photo portrait]."[19] If the repetition of the sign or of the copy constitutes a differentiation that we can rightly define as "extensive," as it deals with a real entity that *is* added to the original entity (and thus gives rise to a serialization), then in the case of presentation it is instead a case of an "intensive" or even *modal* differentiation, one of a different existence than the original, a differentiation that for this reason is not ontic but ontological. The picture is not something added to the original, but shows the original in another form, literally in another mode of its existence.

Truth as Transmutation into Form

The different reality of the picture in comparison to the original, or better, the different reality that the original itself acquires in the picture and its re-presentation, is what Gadamer calls "increase in being" (*Zuwachs an Sein*).[20] This is a concept, at least at first glance, that marks how far Gadamer's notion of the picture is from Plato's, which considered every ontological "duplication" to be a degradation and a distancing from truth. Gadamer, on the contrary, by referring to the neo-Platonic tradition, understood this presumed duplication as an emanation, and in fact not as the sign of a diminution, but of an increase in being. This determinate concept in the Gadamerian view stands at the center of his hermeneutic theory and is presented in the form of *applicatio*. The application does not stand in relation to what is interpreted in the same way a copy is related to the model (of which it would be the faithful or equivalent reproduction), or as its simple reflection, which is more superfluous than a copy; rather, application is something that enriches the model. The reference to Aristotle, whose ethics is celebrated by Gadamer, is in this context meaningful, because it shows the difference between the Platonic conception of mimesis and the Gadamerian one, which has as its background the practical philosophy of Aristotle. For Plato, the realization, that is, the copy of an idea constitutes a moment of being's decrease; for Aristotle, however, the carrying out of the good is not its diminution but an ulterior enrichment, a *perfecting*. Practical philosophy thus assumes a central function within philosophical hermeneutics, because it places the accent on *doing* as a possibility that is not extraneous, but essential for the full consideration of the historical-artistic object. This accentuation of the historical moment is not a deficiency in comparison to the ideal and non-sensible dimension, that is, in comparison to theory, but is instead what gives concreteness and completion, *determinateness*, to experience and to its truth.

Certainly not Platonic in its genesis, this idea of an "increase in being" is clearly neo-Platonic, and pushes Gadamer to reconsider the Plotinian doctrine of emanation:

> Essential to an emanation is that what emanates is an overflow. What it flows from does not thereby become less. The development of this concept by Neoplatonic philosophy, which uses it to get beyond Greek substance ontology, is the basis of the positive ontological status of the picture. For if the original One is not diminished by the overflow of the many from it, this means that being increases.[21]

Gadamer grasps very well the idea that the concept of an increase in being constitutes an overcoming of the Greek substantialist ontology, which is possible only thanks to the elaboration of a modal ontology through the concepts of power, possibility, and act, that open the way to an intensional, and no longer only extensional (as that founded on set theory) conception of reality: reality can present itself in different modes. Among these modes, Aristotle listed also the true and the false. Through the ontology of the picture—which repeats what he had already said regarding the ontology of the work of art—Gadamer intends to elaborate exactly this ontological conception of truth, whose function would be to present the real in a different and higher degree of its being. This increase is the "more" of knowledge. In the picture, actually, the original goes into knowledge, that is, it makes itself *recognizable* as such. The Platonic doctrine of anamnesis expresses this point well, by claiming that the sensible world is the occasion of the awakening of knowledge, and namely of the reactivation of an already possessed knowledge. But, dissociating himself from Plato's general devaluation of representation, Gadamer thinks that in the mimetic representation the original comes "into the There more authentically."[22] Recollecting, then, is not simply calling back to mind something already known, but letting something more about the known object appear. "The joy of recognition is rather the joy of knowing *more* than is already familiar."[23] It is then a question of a real aesthetic experience, and indeed of an experience of joy: the "joy of knowledge."[24] The call to the festival and to play finds here an additional justification: knowledge, at the very end, is the "festival of thought," an experience of fulfillment. "The being of all play is always self-realization, sheer fulfillf ment, *enérgeia* which has its *télos* within itself."[25]

It is true, however, that this positive experience is only one aspect of the experience of truth. It is in fact also possible to experience truth in a negative way, in terms of contradiction or the falsification of our beliefs and prejudices, indeed as suffering (*páthei máthos*).[26] The cosmological experience of alternating between day and night, or in Hegel's terminology, of the rising (*aufgehen*) and the setting (*untergehen*)—which, as we have seen (cf. above, chapter 3), forms the background of the Heideggerian conception of truth—is described by Gadamer from a more subjective point of view, in terms of a "phenomenology" in the Hegelian sense: it becomes the experience of the inversion of knowledge, the experience of the negativity that it tests in the falsification of its certainties and its prejudices, and the experience of its realization and fullness. The reference to Hegel is undeniable, but must not be overstated. In Gadamer, the positive experience of truth can never, as happens in Hegel, be understood as a "synthetic" moment in which the preceding negativity is redeemed and overcome. In fact, there are two moments that remain distinct, and between which it is in fact difficult to perform a synthesis: on the one side, we have the experience of falsification, the Socratic moment of "knowing one does not know" that follows the cancelling out of one's own certainties and the pain that comes with them; on the other side, we have the experience of the fullness of being, of its overabundance, witnessed by the encounter with the work of art, with which our prior certainty is not refuted, but led to apprehend *more* than what was previously understood. To paraphrase Hegel's words, we can consider this former aspect the *negative alethic* moment of truth and the latter as the *positive alethic* moment.

As I said, they do not stand in opposition as thesis and antithesis, but rather as two distinct modalities of experiencing truth.

In both cases the object is, so to speak, "transmuted," is seen "differently": indeed, in knowledge we experience a transmutation of our whole being and of our reality. The limits of substantialist ontology, already shown through the definition of the mimetic relation, emerge here with a new clarity. Actually, the transmutation is not a change of something accidental, an alteration, which leaves the substantial ground of a thing unchanged. It is not a qualitative change that concerns only the categorical dimension of an object, but is an overall transformation that regards its totality, a "transmutation into form" (*Verwandlung ins Gebilde*):[27] "But transmutation means that something is suddenly and as a whole something else, that this other transmuted thing that it has become is its true being, in comparison with which its earlier being is nil."[28]

We understand then that the "more" which produces this transmutation—the "more" which distinguishes the picture from the original, the presentation from what is re-presented, the event of the festival from its first manifest tation—is truth: "With regard to knowledge of the true, the being of the representation is more than the being of the thing represented, Homer's Achilles more than the original."[29] The sentence by which Gadamer synthesizes this point is as concise as it is incisive: "Thus the concept of transmutation characterizes the independent and superior mode of being of what we called form. From this viewpoint 'reality' is defined as what is untrasmuted, and art as the raising up (*Aufhebung*) of this reality into its truth."[30] What is outlined in the Gadamerian theory of play as presentation, of mimesis as the increase in being and of "transmutation into form," is a peculiar relation between reality and truth radically different from the traditional one: neither a correspondence nor a simple making present. These two ways of understanding truth are referable, respectively, to the copy (by which we measure the correspondence to the original) and to specular reflection (which presents the object only insofar as it is present): in both theories truth is conceived as an *external* relation between two entities, between the original and the copy or its reflection. The "transmutation into form" instead helps us to understand the original, that is, reality, as what is not transmutated, and truth as one of its diverse modalities, its increase from the ontological point of view: just when I recognize it for what it is, it does not leave it "just as it is."

This idea of truth as "addition," "increase in being," helps us to understand in a more appropriate way, and certainly not a relativistic one,

Heidegger's well-known claim that Newton's laws were neither true nor false before their discovery. We recognize that gravity was certainly *real* already before its discovery,[31] but the fact that we know it *now* constitutes a different mode of presenting such a reality, precisely in the form of truth. Without the formulation of Newton's laws this different mode of the real would not have been possible: it is an acquisition that elevates the real to the level of knowledge, constituting in it an increase in sense as expressed here by Gadamer.

We can now understand in which sense, from a hermeneutical point of view, the so-called predicate "true" is not redundant: it has a full semantic content, through which we distinguish the real from the truth. That carries with it, as we have said, the taking into account of a position that the real, in itself, does not have and could not have: the reference to the one for whom the truth of the real is presented. This reference is not a psychologization of the truth, but is the ultimate sense of its function, so to speak, "exceeding" in respect to reality. What is true is more than what is real, and this is so because it carries with it a relation to whoever says "this is true." With truth, reality is enriched in the dimension of knowledge, understanding through this the fact that, in it, a knowledge is manifested, something is re-cognized. This is so even with a negative knowledge, namely a knowledge that demonstrated the falsity of a prior belief (or prejudice) about the object rather than the object itself—the Socratic "knowing one does not know."

By arguing against the deflationist conceptions of truth and interpreting the work of Tarski as substantially "partial"—in the sense that it says something about the concept of truth, but not everything—Donald Davidson expresses a similar idea:

> My own view is that Tarski has told us much of what we want to know about the concept of truth, and that there must be more. [. . .] The concept of truth has essential connections with the concepts of belief and meaning, but these connections are untouched by Tarski's work. It is here that we should expect to uncover what we miss in Tarski's characterizations of truth predicates. [. . .] What we need to do now is to say how to identify the presence of such a pattern or structure [of truth] in the behaviour of people.[32]

The whole of these ulterior aspects required by the concept of truth—specifically, knowing and behavior—is what is explicitly theorized in the hermeneutical concept of experience, which leads inevitably to the consideration of the concept of truth as a transformational concept. That is not a definition of truth; rather, it is the consequence of a definitive awareness that, if it is not possible to give any definition of truth,[33] the only way to speak of it is to say what it does, understanding it as a mode, that is, as a transformational operator. To say "it is true that *p*" adds nothing to the content of *p*; but, it is the index of a dispositional *transformation* of whoever assumes such a truth.[34]

Formation as Elevation to an Intensional Universality

Truth is therefore for Gadamer a "more" in comparison to the real, an increase in being. That means that truth in the Gadamerian conception brings with it a "transmutation" of the real, "placing it into form" by making it rise to a superior modality of being. This task can be defined explicitly in ethical terms, that is, as *formation*, which coincides (as we have seen in the discussion of the myth of the cave) with a process of *liberation*.

The Gadamerian recovery of concepts from the humanistic tradition—such as culture, common sense, taste, and judgment—is understood too simply in terms of pure traditionalism, as if it only dealt with the valorization of the mere content carried by those concepts. It is true that Gadamer insists greatly on the substantial aspect of the tradition, which is deposited in the "classic"; this insistence serves as an indication of a normative dimension that is not ahistorical but is constituted in history through its always renewed recognition of human experience, that is, through its continual presentations. What instead seems much more important is the fact that with these concepts—and in particular with the fundamental concept of culture—the formative dimension (*Bildung*) of the human sciences, which *coincides* with their truth-bearing role, is brought to the fore. The formative process is in fact described as the "elevation to humanity" (Herder), that is, as an "increase" of the human reality, a transmutation into a different form. Culture (*Bildung*) is formation, literally, "transmutation into form."

The process of the elevation of humanity is described as a process of uncoupling from the particularity of one's being: "Whoever abandons himself to his particularity is *ungebildet* (unformed)."[35] For Hegel this is a process of abstraction through which one manages to take leave from oneself in order to "rise to the universal."[36] Described in this way, however, the formative process appears to be completely correlative to the logic of abstraction, according to which, the more one is cultivated, the more she "impoverishes" her being, denuding it of its own particularity, in the same way that in the process of abstraction the particular qualities are eliminated in favor of universal ones—ones that are necessarily poorer in terms of their connotations. But this way of understanding formation does not recognize what we have seen associated with the concept of "transmutation into form," namely, the "increase in being." To arrive at this different conception of universality, one has to question the logical rule according to which an always-greater extension corresponds to a gradually decreasing intension: on the contrary, the universal which elevates the cultured human is that of an always-greater intensional richness; not a process of abstraction, but a process of inclusion. The cultured human is the one who, having seen and understood much, having lived many experiences, has learned from them that sensibility by which one can always *understand* more of oneself and others. The universality that elevates is not an abstract one that consists in the exclusion but in the inclusion of the greatest possible number of particularities in one's life. Formation, therefore, as a transmutation into form, is the achievement of a human condition that is "more true" because it is richer experientially, which results not from an ever-greater purification from differences—according to that process of abstraction that guides the scientific consciousness as the reduction of phenomena to general laws—but through a totality of differences. This type of universality is thus radically distinct from the reductive one inherited from formal logic, whose law is the inverse relation between extension and intension: the smaller its number of characteristics, the greater its universality. On the contrary, the universality dealt with here is the fruit of a law of direct proportionality between extension and intension: the greater its number of intensional specifications, the greater its universality. This law is at its core that of the Hegelian logic, which is a logic of experience: in experience nothing is erased, and its universality is the result of its always-greater intensional richness.

Moreover, the greater this richness the more it is able to accommodate the other, and in this sense it is, precisely because it is "more universal," even "more true." The term "opening," which is often used to name the hermeneutic conception of truth, thus takes on very well its various implications, which are limited neither to the ontological dimension (the opening as "clearing," the space in which the manifestation of entities is made possible) nor to the epistemological (the opening as paradigm or world view), but also and above all include the ethical dimension, to which the problem of cultural universality is always referred. "Knowing that one does not know" is not a closing, but is the availability for new experiences and new truths: "The dialectic of experience has its proper fulfillment not in definitive knowledge but in the openness to experience that is made possible by experience itself."[37] The result is a *humanity* inconceivable in terms of extensional universality—that is, in terms of a substantial core shared by all humans that constitutes the source of their identity—and instead thought in terms of an intensional universality, that is, as a sum of differences: the human being *understands* the other because it is open to the other. The victory of this universality is thus the extreme result of the defense of the content of truth of the human sciences against the claim to reduce, in general, truth to the certainty of method, that is, to the abstracting universalization of methodological consciousness: "The hermeneutical consciousness culminates not in methodological sureness of itself, but in the same readiness for experience that distinguishes the experienced man from the man captivated by dogma."[38] The experienced human is the one who through experience learns to be more open by thus becoming "more universal": it is a human being *free* for experience, open to experience, and thus open *to* truth. The truth of the human sciences is that truth which allows us to be elevated to this sort of universality.

Chapter 6

The Sense of Truth

Force and Interpretation

The idea of a transformative power of truth is situated within a general conception of language according to which—and contrary to the tradition that, since Aristotle, has assigned it a primarily descriptive function—it possesses its own force, that is, a capacity to produce determinate effects.[1] Every saying, as Austin writes, is thus also a doing; it is bestowed with an effectual power, which ranges from simple informing about something ordinary, to swearing, committing, and even inducing determinate behaviors in the interlocutor, as happens primarily in the poetic-rhetorical functions of language, such as to convince, to persuade, to surprise, and to astound. This energetic conception of language, which above all dwells on the analysis of its objective side, namely, on the *things* that it does with words, nevertheless assumes a very different radicality in an author like Nietzsche, who refers everything back to force. Nietzsche developed an energetics of language in a grandiose way by instead analyzing it from the subjective side, tracing every expression back to force, that is, to the will from which it originates. Gilles Deleuze highlights this aspect of Nietzsche's philosophy in a particular way, clearly seeing in Nietzsche a figure who continues the metaphysics of force that in the modern era had its most important proponents in Leibniz and Spinoza. According to Deleuze, force is what Nietzsche understands by the word "sense":

> We will never find the sense of something (of a human, a biological or even a physical phenomenon) if we do not know the force which appropriates the thing, which exploits it, which takes possession of it or is expressed in it. [. . .] Nietzsche substitutes the correlation of sense and phenomenon for the metaphysical duality of appearance and essence and for the scientific relation of cause and effect.[2]

This force is the origin of value, and thus of the valuation that follows it. If nothing is neutral, it is because there is always a force that actively appropriates it in the moment. Everything can therefore acquire different senses according to the force that takes possession of it: "Thus, in a favourite example of Nietzsche's, religion does not have a unique sense, it serves many forces."[3] Nevertheless, the essence of religion is given by the prevailing force that more constantly shapes and determines it.

The task of interpretation is the search for the force instilled in an assertion or a value. "To interpret" for Nietzsche means bringing something back to its sense, namely, to the force from which it originates. In short, interpretation has a clear genealogical intention, deriving from the properly philosophical inflection that Nietzsche grants to philology, as the study of cultural objects and their transformation that follows the modes of their production and their historical transmission.[4]

The correlation between force and sense underlined by Deleuze is precisely what allows this thesis to be reformulated and focused in a different way, so as to avoid the error of will, or even worse, violence, that seems to be derived from it: what Nietzsche calls force is nothing other than the *mode* with which an assertion, and in general an act, is completed. If the illocutionary force about which philosophy speaks in speech act theory corresponds to the intentionality that can be associated with a determinate locutionary act, what Nietzsche is addressing is most often something non-intentional, a "will" in the Schopenhauerean sense of the term, or even a more or less unconscious force that is expressed in a determinate formation of meaning. This is a mode, a "how," that we might say is *transcendental* and that regards the conditions of possibility of the sense of our knowledge, assertions, beliefs, and actions.

Understood in this way, interpretation is *critical*, as it is aimed at highlighting these "a priori forms." Critical, I would say, in a sense that is very Kantian and perhaps even more radical than Kantian critique. In fact, Deleuze observes that for Nietzsche it is neither a matter of conducting a critique of values in the name of other values, that is, of contesting a value on the basis of a differing or opposed value—that is what the "philosophical laborers" do[5]—nor a critique that annuls them by referring them back to something else more objective from which they were derived, to facts, as utilitarians and scholars do; rather, it is a matter of thinking the strict correlation between values and force—namely, the modality—that is expressed in them: an *adverbial* dimension that precedes and grounds, genealogically, the dimension of objects: "There are things that can only be said, felt or conceived, values which can only be adhered to, on condition of 'base' evaluation, 'base' living and thinking."[6] What Nietzsche presents here could be defined an "adverbial transcendentalism": force, or sense, is the relational modality that defines or determines a certain *quid*, a given value or a given meaning.

This distinction from Deleuze, which highlights the critical character of the genealogical method, and therefore of the interpretation of which it makes use, recalls some considerations one also finds in Kant when he speaks of his critical method. It is true that for Kant critique also has a juridical-procedural meaning, as the "tribunal of reason" that must estimate and define its limits and its claims, an aspect that is foreign to the genealogical method. Nevertheless, for Kant and for Nietzsche, critique is such because it *is not about its contents*, but their legitimacy, or better, their genesis. The transcendental deduction is the essence of critique as it exposes the "birth certificate" of the concepts that does not show their truth, but estimates the possibility of their truth. What brings together the Kantian and the Nietzschean procedures is therefore not a shared goal, but rather the point where critique takes shape—namely, in the relation of the representation to its object.

This aspect appears particularly clear where, in a passage from the first edition of the transcendental Dialectic dedicated to the Paralogisms of pure Psychology, Kant distinguishes *dogmatic objections* from *critical objections*:

> The dogmatical attacks the proposition, the critical the proof of a proposition. The former presupposes an insight into the peculiar nature of the object in order to be able to assert the contrary of what the proposition asserts. It is therefore itself dogmatical, and pretends to know the peculiar nature of the object in question better than the opponent. The critical objection, as it says nothing about the worth or worthlessness of the proposition, and attacks the proof only, need not know the object itself better, or claim a better knowledge of it. All it wants to show is, that a proposition is not well grounded, not that it is false.[7]

The dogmatic procedure in general is characterized by the attention to the content, to what is said, and puts forward its arguments by opposing one content to another (the world is finite, the world is not finite): the dogmatic objection thus claims to know the nature of things better than its adversary; the critical procedure instead focuses on the *mode* in which a determinate affirmation is conducted: the proposition is left to its value or lack of value, and does not claim to know the object better, but interrogates its "conditions of possibility."

An Experimental Ontology

Nietzsche's genealogical method is undeniably connected to this idea of critique: it is not so much a matter of opposing one thesis to another, as it is the interrogation of its genesis, that is, its originating force, its sense. *The Birth of Tragedy* also called this sense *spirit*: Apollonian and Dionysian are the two modalities, the two possible senses, of feeling Greek—the forces that had shaped Greekness and had produced the works that we all know. But the most important consequence of this genealogical method, of its critical force, is that it does not lead to the refutation of theories believed to be erroneous, but rather to a different way of living. Vattimo writes,

> the culturally critical and demystifying philosophy which Nietzsche developed in his "middle period" is a philosophy relatively "free" of positive theorizing. In fact, it lacks those "results" which would be obtained from going beyond the setting out of an "intellectual attitude."[8]

Aphorism 20 of *Human, All Too Human* clarifies this aspect through the idea of the "movement backwards," that is, the capacity to understand "the historical justification that resides in such ideas, likewise the psychological" that is the basis of cultural formations.[9] The idea that every positive metaphysics (dogmatic metaphysics, in Kant's terms) might be an error is only a half-negative: the understanding of genesis, namely interpretation, must lead to a new temperament that does not display "snarling and sullenness—those familiar tedious qualities of old dogs and men who have long been kept on the leash."[10] Thus, there is no positive definition of the "free spirit." Vattimo also writes that the philosophy of the morning "remains the definition of an attitude, a spiritual climate, not a philosophical 'doctrine' in the strict sense."[11]

But what does all of this entail in the passage from the critical dimension to the later Nietzsche's attempt to elaborate—above all as it appeared to Heidegger—a real philosophy, indeed an ontology? The question first of all concerns the very definition of ontology, which ever since Kant's critique has been in need of a redefinition: it no longer concerns the description of what there is (as in its metaphysical meaning), but the definition of its conditions of possibility (and this is its new critical meaning). In the same way for Nietzsche, ontology is not concerned with what there is, but with what could be there. It necessarily has—and this was missed by Heidegger, but is grasped well by Vattimo—an experimental, hypothetical, and thus creative (or better, transformative) dimension.

Nietzsche's theorization of nihilism is therefore not an ontology in the traditional sense, but an *experimental* ontology that leads to the production of something new by inducing determinate actions and reactions of force. If the genealogy works by means of chemical reductions, as stated in the first aphorism of *Human, All Too Human*, the ontology that counterbalances it also arises through chemical reactions. The overman is the result of this experiment, dramatized in the story about the death of God told by Zarathustra, the result of an alchemic experiment that ablates and cancels out all of the forces that characterize the Platonic-Christian individual: ressentiment, bad conscience, the need to submit, humility.

The singling out of these existential modalities is therefore what "establishes" values, that is, the particular meanings that we produce: the conditions of possibility of the objects of experience—understood in its broader meaning, and not in a merely genealogical one—as the conditions of possibility of our own experiencing in general. If our values have a *pudenda origo*, the discovery of which heightens its insignificance, if existence itself is discovered to be lacking in meaning,[12] it is because existence cannot be estimated on its own. Existence is the source of values which are originated by modes of being, of existing. As such, existence cannot for its part be judged according to them.

Deleuze emphasized the radicality of this position by arguing that it was Nietzsche, not Kant, who carried out critique to its end, precisely because Kant did not know how to pose the problem in terms of values. He was thus confined to critique of this or that truth, their conditions of possibility, but never the very possibility of truth itself. To raise this question means, for Nietzsche, to pose the problem of the *modality* of truth, that is, the *sense* of truth, of its possible senses. Nietzsche had often, though not always, seen a nihilistic will at the core of the will to truth—negator of life and of the joy of living. But, as we have observed, from the moment that the sense of a phenomenon can be multiple, rather than univocal—such that one could also speak here of a "method of variations" for discerning in them the reciprocal interdependencies between the sense and the phenomenon, in the manner that Husserl had spoken of them—the question that is now raised is *whether or not a non-nihilistic sense of truth exists.*

For Whom Is Truth?

Paragraph 424 of *Daybreak* offers more than a hint in this direction. Its title is "For Whom the Truth Exists." It deals with the principal question of the genealogical method, which in contrast to the metaphysical method asks, "who is?" rather than "what is?" It is thus not a matter of asking "what is truth?" but "who is the one to whom truth refers?": who is the sort of human to whom truth is granted, the existential modality who is associated with truth, or called upon by it?

Nietzsche's response is surprising. In the first part of the aphorism he rails against the utilitarian conception of truth: the idea that truth *serves* something and that it *ought* to serve someone—that its sense might be to bring comfort to humanity. But, Nietzsche asks himself, what could the truth ever have in common "with the inner states of suffering, stunted, sick human beings that they must necessarily be of use to them?"[13] Even though critique always points to the "who" of every formation of meaning, that does not mean that it is the *utilitarian* term of this genealogical director; rather, this critical reference to the "who" has the same sense as the Kantian reference to the "I think," which must be able to accompany every one of my representations so that an experience can be given. This reference remains completely formal, however, and is specified through the modalities that are the very constitution of human experience: space, time, and the categories. In the same way, the Nietzschean reference to the "who" of values can take on various modalities, among which the utilitarian is but *one* of the possible variations. What constitutes the fertile ground of nihilism, the humus of the need for comfort that it is disposed to, and takes for truth everything and only that which responds to this need, is the strong

> conviction that mankind was the goal of nature, [so that] it was assumed without question that nothing could be disclosed by knowledge that was not salutary and useful to man, indeed that things other than this *could* not, *ought* not to *exist*.[14]

In this way, the alleged truth is constituted as a comforting world of fiction: "up to now errors have been forces of *consolation*."

Consequently, the lie is nothing in the end but self-deception: the construction of a fictional world is the response to a need for consolation, and thus an unconscious attempt at self-deception. Nihilism is born in this way. The construction of an otherworldly world responds to a need to find a consolation in it, for the impossibility—or incapacity—of accepting this world, of saying Yes to the earth.

And so, for whom is truth, if its negation is in reality the result of illness, fear, and absence of joy?

> Perhaps all this leads to the proposition that truth, *as a whole* and interconnectedly, exists only for souls which are at once powerful and harmless, and full of joyfulness and peace (as was the soul of Aristotle), just as it will no doubt be only such souls as these that will be capable of *seeking it*: for, no matter how proud they may be of their intellect and its freedom, the others are seeking *cures* for themselves—they are *not* seeking truth. This is why these others take so little real pleasure in science, and make of the coldness, dryness and inhumanity of science a reproach to it: it is the sick passing judgment on the games of the healthy.[15]

There is therefore an essential opposition between two modes of considering truth and two modes of being, two typologies of man. For the former, truth would be a sort of consolation, a remedy, a medicine, a *phármakon*, and to this would correspond a type of human who is ill, not free, enslaved; for this type of human God is like a doctor[16] who is obeyed blindly for pure moralism, because "God ordains!" For the latter, truth is instead a joyous, disinterested experience, one made for strong, healthy spirits who have no need for consolation and do not expect it. This is truth in the extra-moral sense, if, as Nietzsche writes frequently, morality is nothing other than the expression of an ill spirit.

The idea that truth is merely a convention kept in place in order to avoid the *bellum omnium contra omnes*—an act of avoiding aggression that consists in the acceptance of a shared simulation, "a mobile army of metaphors, metonymies, anthropomorphisms, in short a sum of human relations [that,] after they have been in use a long time, strike people as firmly established, canonical, and binding"[17] illusions or worn-out metaphors, as Nietzsche writes in "On Truth and Lies in a Nonmoral Sense,"[18]—corresponds to the unavoidable inclination of humans to let themselves be deceived. Is this an essential human characteristic from which the equally essential definition of truth as a "necessary falsehood" is derived?

The transformability of the human, affirmed by the doctrine of the overman, also entails the transformability of the human relation with truth, which is no longer a *therapeutic* relation, but a joyous relation that renders science joyous, gay. Rarely has truth been wed to joy in the history of philosophy: historicism, according to Nietzsche, is the most emblematic example of how the pathos for knowledge goes hand in hand with the negation of life. One cannot think, however, that the concept of truth is *in itself* a nihilistic concept: as with every other value, its sense depends on the will that appropriates it and expresses it. In the end, what Nietzsche says about morals can also be said about truth, namely, that it is not a matter of denying that moral or immoral actions exist, but of completely changing our relation with them. "We have *to learn to think differently*—in order at last, perhaps very late on, to attain even more: *to feel differently*."[19]

Truth is therefore not a concept in itself *nihilistic*; and perhaps there aren't any concepts that are nihilistic *in themselves:* "nihilistic" denotes a way of feeling about the objects to which it refers and the concepts that it employs. Here one finds the emptiness of Nietzsche's theoretical proposal, as Vattimo confirms—an emptiness that is the invitation to experience new, freer, and more joyous modes of being: "it is not enough to bring about a doctrine," Nietzsche writes in a note from the autumn of 1883, "men also have to be *violently transformed* in order to agree to it!—This is what Zarathustra ultimately understands."[20] The doctrine of the eternal return is the *experiment* that Zarathustra proposes for testing humans and assaying their capacity for transformation because the form of the eternal return is the very form of truth, the form of the tautological, unmodifiable return. The eternal return is the experiment that assays our relation to truth, the "litmus test" that identifies the chemical component conditioning our relation with truth, telling us if it is "acidic" or "alkaline," nihilistic or joyous. The test provokes, and thus makes manifest, the *reaction* in its confrontations: whoever cannot bear the eternal return is the sick human who seeks consolation from truth and thus does not know how to have a *free* relation with it; whoever can bear it is a spirit that is disinterested and powerful, joyous and calm, like Aristotle, free from ressentiment when faced with life, and thus not in need of consolation.[21] Nietzsche writes in *Human, All Too Human* that the decision about the effect of knowledge is "determined by a man's *temperament*."[22]

What therefore seems to me important to emphasize is the particular relation, nondogmatic but critical, that Nietzsche has with theories and philosophical doctrines. The same nihilism would risk being a new dogmatism if it were identified fundamentally on the level of content. But there are no nihilistic contents *in themselves*. Just as a human is not honest due to that obscure quality we call "honesty," but rather due to his individual and concrete behaviors,[23] so too there is no "nihilistic" quality belonging to concepts. This critical operation is compared to a process of inversion by Deleuze, similar to what Marx does in relation to Hegel:

> Finally, Nietzsche's relation to Kant is like Marx's to Hegel: Nietzsche stands critique on its feet, just as Marx does with the dialectic. But this analogy, far from reconciling Marx and Nietzsche, separates them still further. For the dialectic comes from the original Kantian form of critique. There would have been no need to put the dialectic back on its feet, nor "to do" any form of dialectics if critique itself had not been standing on its head from the start.[24]

The need to refer every value to the force from which it originates, to identify its germinal sense, to ask who is always there at the source of a certain formulation of meaning is therefore, in the end, Nietzsche's intention, a way of not remaining prisoners of the world of abstractions, of theories, of doctrines, but of returning to the earth, that is, to the effective terrain of experience. The overman, the one capable of being free, of a joyous existence, of accepting life, and truth, is perhaps simply a person who no longer walks with his head down. To use the words of Marx, that person is not alienated.

Chapter 7

A Non-alienated Conception of Truth

The Form of Truth: Truth and Experiential Realism

In the previous chapters we saw that the problem of truth always entails a reference to the "who" of the sentence. This reference, more than a subjectivization, is instead the result of a structural complication due to the traditional way of setting up the problem of truth in terms of what I would call "experiential realism," which is distinct not only from metaphysical realism, but also from empirical realism.

According to Hilary Putnam's definition, metaphysical realism consists in the assertion of a reality in itself, completely independent of our consciousness, and of which there is only one true and complete description.[1] The word "true" in this case is nothing other than the sign of such independence: it would sanction the total autonomy of reality, placing an abyss between it and us. If we say that something is true, in short, it is as if we were describing a state of affairs even if we ourselves, who speak and hear that sentence, do not exist at all. In this way truth would constitute the very condition of every essence, that is, of objects and of a world in itself. Independence from experience is thus the typical characteristic of the metaphysical conception of truth. It is a logical abstraction that, paradoxically, is called *realism,* and that gives rise to what Putnam calls the "*alienated* views of truth":

> they cause one to lose one part or another of one's self and the world, to see the world as simply consisting of elementary particles swerving in the void (the "physicalist" view, which sees the scientific description as converging to the One True Theory), or to see the world as simply consisting of "actual and possible sense-data" (the older empiricist view), or to deny that there is a world at all, as opposed to a bunch of stories that we make up for various (mainly unconscious) reasons.[2]

Both metaphysical realism and also empirical realism (which considers the sensorial datum to be the foundation of consciousness), as with subjectivism or idealism, wind up presenting a unilateral picture of our real experience, or to put it in Heideggerian terms, our being-in-the-world. In opposition to such a conception, philosophical hermeneutics—with its stubborn defense against scientific reductionism of the claim to truth of the human sciences—advances a non-alienated (and thus structurally more complex) picture of truth.

The alienation of the conception of truth belonging to the aforementioned theories consists therefore in the fact that they would force us to dispense with some piece of the world: the I, its objectivations, or external reality. This formal simplification, close to reductionism, would in logic correspond to the consideration of "true" as a monadic predicate representing God's point of view, that is, a "No Eye view of truth,"[3] and thus definitively the point of view of no one (what a view from no eye might be is a picture that is somewhat unintelligible). We can thus consider metaphysical realism to be the theory that thinks the predicate of truth as monadic.[4] The dogmatic character—in the Kantian sense of the term—of metaphysical realism appears clearly in its making reference to a conception of reality that, in principle, no one will be able to verify (or, even worse, will be able to falsify); in fact, how could one verify that the world should be as it is even without anyone who could see it, observe it, think about it, and make judgments about it? *Who* will ever be able to make an assertion of that sort and assume it to be true?[5] For a metaphysical realist, a true description could also have no one in a position to describe it (it is a description of a "no place"); for an experiential (not metaphysical) realist, instead, anyone can be in a position to describe it, but never no one.

Gadamer thematized this necessary reference to an observer by taking as a model the concept of play, whose openness to the spectator is essential, since play acquires its full significance only thanks to the spectator. Play is always a "representation for someone."[6] In this sense, play describes the aesthetic experience and, in fact, experience in general, and even the being of nature. The principal characteristic of play is self-presentation, and "self-presentation is a universal ontological characteristic of nature."[7] Thanks to the spectator, what is presented assumes the *form* of truth, because only in this way is it "for someone" who can know it and recognize it as such. There would be no truth without this contribution of the spectator because there would not be any experience of the real. The experience of the real is the necessary condition (of the experience) of truth. In short, this not only means that truth is always *for* someone, but that *reality, as true, is for someone.*

What distinguishes this "being for" from relativism is precisely the fact that such a relation is not considered a sufficient condition of truth (that something is true because it is for me), but only expresses its necessary condition (there is truth only because there is Dasein, as Heidegger says). The structure of "for someone" ultimately expresses a *formal* condition of truth, which in sentences such as "it is true that *p*" is understood as necessary inasmuch as it can be omitted from the sentence. On the contrary, every mere "for me" *must* be expressed in the sentence (that does not exclude the elliptical relation to an "I-think").[8] I would call this structure of truth, involving an elliptical reference to its deictic condition of possibility, "Convention-E." It is in fact expressed by the Heideggerian phrase that we have cited many times: "there is truth in so far as Dasein is." This conditional statement expresses the idea that, for hermeneutics, the presupposition of every truth is Dasein.

"Convention-E" states the relation between Dasein, that is Existence, and truth as an *agreement*: *convenientia* is, not surprisingly, one of the ways that truth has been defined in the tradition. As I have tried to argue elsewhere, the term points out the *accidentality* of such a relation. The relation between Dasein and truth is not therefore an analytic implication, but a sort of "a priori synthesis" according to which Dasein and truth come together without being originarily dependent on each other.[9] The term *convenientia* can then be considered a translation of the Greek term *symbebekós*, from the verb *symbaínein*, literally "to come with, to agree."

This *convenientia* of Dasein and truth is thus in a certain sense the "a priori synthesis" that describes the transcendental form of experience for Kant. It assumes definitively the same value in Kantian critique as the reference to experience, in which the assertion of a "truth in itself," beyond possible experience, is considered to be a form of dogmatism. The assumption of a reality that can be called "true" without one that can talk about it or observe it, therefore, is the constitutive dogma of metaphysical realism; but, by depriving itself of the reference to experience, it saws off the branch on which it is sitting. Truth is not a state of the real *independently* of its being accessible, but is a state of the real *made accessible* for a subject that has an experience of it.

If being-true is not a one-place predicate—which would carry a high price in terms of the alienation of its concept—it must be conceived as a predicate of at least two (or more) places, that is, as some sort of relation. The profound sense of Kant's critical revolution consists in having undertaken such a transformation of monadic concepts in general (for example, those that define the primary qualities) by referring them implicitly to the "I think," namely, to that transcendental condition that defines the *form* of a possible experience. The conception of truth as correspondence—which Kant, according to Heidegger, establishes for the first time—in fact constitutes a first step in this direction, since it turns truth precisely into a relation, and not into a monadic predicate. Thomas Aquinas had already understood this: if in fact, on the one hand, he claimed that the true coincides with what there is, and thus is defined as a property that inheres to the thing itself, on the other hand, he also observed that it shapes the relation of the intellect to the thing, and is thus *ratio*, namely, a relation.[10] This formal relation, distinct from the relation of identity that assimilates *esse* and *verum*, is the foundation of the conception of truth as adequation or correspondence between the intellect and the thing. It thus *adds* something to the pure tautology of "being = true," even though this addition might not be anything that concerns the thing itself, but only the relation of it to the intellect. This "addition" is in short what makes the predicate "true" (which it would be wrong to call a "predicate"): a *mode*; it is, as a matter of fact, the addition not of an ulterior quality to the object, but of an ulterior relational modality between the object and the subject. Or still better, it is the expression of an ulterior state of the real—that of knowing.

The conception of truth as correspondence, considered proper to metaphysical realism, leads to its overcoming by virtue of its very own formal structure: it would be a relation "between words or thought-signs and external things and sets of things."[11] But if truth in metaphysical realism is a monadic relation, a sort of "self-identity," which in principle excludes the relation to a mind, it is hard to see how it might be compatible with correspondence. If there is something positive in the notion of truth as "correspondence," it is then precisely the fact that it exposes the irreducibly relational character of truth, whose form consists in the placing into relation (at least) two elements, the intellect and the thing, the judgment and the state of affairs, the subject and the object, the I and the world.[12] What this notion implicates, in every way, is that if truth is a correspondence, and if there are words, signs or thoughts that are made true by extra-linguistic entities, then there must be someone who speaks and thinks them. For Heidegger, as was said earlier (see chapter 3), the definition of truth as correspondence is not totally wrong, but derivative: it is derivative precisely because by implicating a reference to a Who, it implicitly alludes to a deeper dimension, to that ontological presupposition that Heidegger calls openness and that coincides with the very existence of Dasein.

Against the Equivalence-Thesis

In chapters 2 and 3 we examined the relation between truth and time, both from a formal point of view, by highlighting how the deictic reference to the speaker is essential to the *formulation* of every true judgment, and also from an experiential point of view, by bringing out how the very content of the experience of truth, understood as *alétheia*, is time. This point seems to me the most important contribution of the hermeneutic conception of truth: *alétheia* does not allude to an eternal presentness, to a "being present," but to the phenomenon of coming to be, of "becoming present," and thus to the profound experience of the real as time. The mode of the real that truth shows is temporality.

Such an assertion can also be considered to be the result of the critique of the distinction between ideal and real that, on the one hand, constitutes the implicit presupposition of all of the conceptions of truth as the property of a reality in itself, untouched by our experience, and on the other hand, the target of every conception (from Kant to Heidegger) that instead sees there exactly what connects us to the real. The question was posed in an exemplary manner by Husserl in the pages of the *Prolegomena* to the *Logical Investigations*, where he opposes the psychologism of Sigwart and its relativistic implications by defending a Platonic-objectivistic conception of truth based on the clear distinction between the ideal and the real. To make truth depend on the realization of determinate acts (apprehension, knowing, etc.) means exposing it to annihilation, whereas truth is and remains such regardless of whether such acts are ever realized:

> If there are no intelligent beings, if the natural order excludes them, or if they are, in a *real* sense, impossible—or if there are no beings capable of knowing certain classes of truths—then such *ideal* possibilities remain without fulfilling actually. The apprehension, knowledge, bringing to consciousness of truth (or of certain classes of truths), is nowhere ever realized. Each truth, however, remains in itself what it is, it retains its ideal being: it does not hang somewhere in the void, but is a case of validity in the timeless realm of Ideas. It belongs to the realm of the absolutely valid, into which we fit all cases of validity into which we have *insight* or at least well-founded surmises, and in which we further locate the vaguely presented range of things indirectly and

> indefinitely thought valid, i.e. the cases of validity not as yet known to us, and perhaps never to be known.[13]

The consequence of this conception of truth is its leveling to reality: "true" means real, which leads logically to the so-called thesis of equivalence, that is, to the idea that "it is true that *p*" equals *p*. Such a thesis thus renders the predicate "true" completely useless, since it does nothing more than lower the level where one says "it is true that *p*" to the level where there is simply *p*. This tautology is the "self-identity" which stretches metaphysical realism's notion of truth. On the contrary, the distinction between the simple *p* and "it is true that *p*" seems to me to be the core of the Gadamerian conception of truth (as we have seen in chapters 4 and 5). For Gadamer, to say that "it is true that *p*" means saying something not only about the real, but also about our being in the world, and in particular revealing that an important and meaningful thing happened in our experience. It is *historical* truth that precedes even the nomological truth of science, in which the event is considered the expression of a law, that is, the moment of an essential truth. The truth of the law is surely objective, but of an abstract objectivity because it deliberately leaves aside the objectivity of the event: the event produces a real effect, such that without it the world would not be what it is. This distinction between the objectivity of the law and that of the event is the distinction that we have already seen in the meaning of the term *alétheia*, between the objectivity of essence and the objectivity of existence, which *implicates* the dimension of time.

Time in fact marks—as is clear from the preceding quotation from Husserl—the abyss between the ideal and the real, essence and existence, *realitas* and *actualitas*: the world of truth would stand on the side of atemporal ideality. Temporal experience—which is always the experience of existences—is thus reduced to something optional and dispensable. On the contrary, if one assumes that the very form of truth cannot not implicate time, and therefore that its experiential content is always implicitly a temporal thing (that is *also* true of scientific experience), even this distinction falls apart. What is true in this case does not distinguish itself from the real because it is *without time*, and thus ideal, but distinguishes itself from it because it is only a *different* conformation of the real, made possible precisely by time. Time is thus not the condition of the impossibility of truth, but, according to the critical logic of the Kantian variety—a logic that inverts or redefines determinate relations of presupposition or of incompatibility as they are conceptualized by the old metaphysics or by dogmatic rationalism—it is in fact its very condition of possibility.

The fact that the word "true" alludes to such an experience—which, ultimately, is the most banal and radical experience that we can have, the experience of time as the experience of the formal condition of every other experience—constitutes its semantic richness. The reversal of this dimension is the reason the meaning of the word "true" is lost in many deflationist theories, where the same form of metaphysical realism that we discussed earlier acts under the surface. On the contrary, to understand truth as "increase in being" is a mode of expressing the semantic weight and explicating at the same time the metalinguistic character of "true"—the fact, namely, that it does not belong to the object language.[14] The experience of reality is more than reality, because only by having the experience of the real can we speak of the true and the false.

The defense of the monadic character of truth must respond to the problem of *how* (namely, to which conditions) such a predicate is applied to propositions: if it is *left out* of every experience, then the assertion of truth is equated to the real and leads to the "dissolving" of truth on the level of the language-object; if instead it requires experience (which in my view is expressed by its metalinguistic character), then truth is structurally "for" someone and assumes a transcendental character. More than a semantic ascent, the metalinguisticality of truth would therefore mean a "semantic descent" from theory—or from language—to experience.

The expression "experience of truth" thus alludes to the fact that the *formal* structuring of truth can only be the structuring of experience itself, summed up in what we have called "Convention-E." In fact, the ontological-existential declination that Heidegger confers on the problem of truth consists in considering truth as the constitutive nexus of our being-in-the-world. Truth (as *alétheia*) is the form itself of being-in, which is a unitary relation thanks to which a Who is "in the world" and exists. A non-alienated view of truth cannot *not* carry with it such a structural connection between the world and the one Who is in the world. Far from being something semantically empty and redundant, truth therefore expresses—from the point of view of philosophical hermeneutics—something that has a decisive and undeniable value on the experiential level: philosophical hermeneutics opposes to the deflationist conception of truth, which seems to me completely consubstantial to every realistic conception of truth (which considers "true" to be a predicate of a *res*), a revaluation rather than a negation of truth (when it also might be understood as correspondence), as the indication of a transmutation within experience. "True" and "false" belong to an intensive, *modal* dimension of experience, since they express the dispositional variations of our relation with the real.

Beyond Domination: Truth as Countervailing Power

To say that truth has a primarily intensive value signifies emphasizing its expressive character more than its representational one (in the sense of *Vorstellung*). Against this idea, the conception of truth as adequation is repeatedly reasserted by underlining the privileged relation that the predicate of truth would institute between our sentences and the facts of the world, not polluted by ethical or intentional considerations. To say that something is true means saying *simply* that it corresponds to reality, that it says or shows something as it is. Truth would thus be a sort of biunivocal relation between the elements of our representations and the things in the world for which they stand. The conception of truth as adequation would thus be only another way of saying that the predicate "true" is the indicator of an equivalence: something in the world corresponds, in a punctual and univocal manner, to what is in the sentence.

The difficulties encountered when one attempts to stabilize more precisely what makes up the relation of correspondence are, however, well known. As we have tried to show (chapter 2), the sentence presents at the same time an excess in respect to what there is in the world, and an ellipsis, because no sentence can ever completely present its own presuppositions of sense. In both cases, what exceeds the sentence's dimension of representation defines a broader horizon, which we can call pragmatic, because in general it concerns the relation of the sentence with the context or with the relative acts or behaviors. This extension to the pragmatic dimension constitutes the horizon of the hermeneutic conception of truth.

On the level of praxis, the function of truth is no longer understood in terms of representation—that is, as a relation of mere correspondence between linguistic elements and extra-linguistic elements—but in energetic terms, namely, as inserted into a "field of forces" that it influences and yet by which, at the same time, it is influenced. In this sense, as Frédéric Gros wrote, it is no longer a mode of organizing discourses, but a principle of the vectorization of existences.[15] This means that truth is granted an effectual power capable of orienting existence, which can be understood in two ways.

On the one hand, in the sense that it is capable of producing transformations: "knowledge is power," Bacon wrote, and this assertion can be understood as the negation of the privileged bond that truth would have with representation—that is, with the pure reflexive contemplation of the real—by singling out in praxis its sphere of highly important action. But, on the other hand, this bond between truth and praxis can be understood in terms of a production of truth *by* power, according to a formula that is the inverse of the one already cited from Bacon: "power is knowledge," that is, power produces truths through devices of control and subjugation. In the first case, it is truth that confers a certain power; in the other, it is power that is subservient to truth, exploiting the power of vectorization and inserting it between itself and existences. What changes in the two cases is the position of power: posterior to truth in the first case, anterior to truth in the second. In the first case we therefore speak more simply of "power," and in the second case of "domination."

As is known, the connection between truth and power was one of the central themes in the reflections of Michel Foucault.[16] The idea of a "truth-phobic"[17] Foucault, who would identify truth with domination without any exception, and which might therefore in this way indicate truth precisely as the principle target of every movement of liberation—truth and freedom being in this way completely incompatible—is destined to be corrected above all in light of his later writings and seminars.[18] In these texts a distinction clearly emerges that allows Foucault to separate domination and truth, in a manner such that truth is no longer useful to domination—that is, as a means of repressive and oppressive practices—but on the contrary becomes an element of resistance against domination: it deals with the distinction between philosophy and spirituality. Philosophy is identified with the practice of controlling truth. This practice is affirmed in Ancient Greece, beginning with Socrates and Plato, and is marked by the translation of the very place of truth from the care of self (*epimeleía heautoû*)—by that praxis turned to an attention and transformation of the subject in its fullness—to discourse. According to Foucault this caused the search for truth to be increasingly identified with the search for its "discursive conditions of possibility," so that the order of the discourse might become the dominant moment in the definition and consideration of truth. This moment finds its completion in Descartes, who on the one hand definitively reduced the realm of the care of self to the sphere of consciousness and, on the other hand, institutionalized this sphere through the elaboration of a precise method for accessing truth. These two reductive movements have led to the identification of truth with rationality, namely, with the power of domination over the real.

The most important consequence of this philosophical reduction of truth to rationality is the exclusion of the formative—or better, transformative—moment by the care of self: the necessary education for gaining access to truth does not require any transformation on the part of the subject but only a "training" in the methodical practices of the scientific community.[19] The abstract nature of these practices is understood as a guarantee of knowledge's objectivity, so that truth can now be conceived as completely unchained from any subjectivity: the process of knowing does not involve the subject but instead tends to exclude it. What is important is the method, not the Self. The metaphysical correlate of this superiority of method (the order of the discourse) over truth is thus that alienated view of truth that Putnam attributes to metaphysical realism, since only the idea that truth might be able to subsist without the knowing subject—which defines the structure of metaphysical realism—can fully ensure its objectivity.

The mode in which the relation to truth was conceived in ancient Greece, according to Foucault, placed the accent on the transformative power of truth, and by involving a human being's entire existence, the experience of truth was instead a "spiritual" experience. Spirituality is

> the search, practice, and experience through which the subject carries out the necessary transformations on himself in order to have access to the truth. We will call "spirituality" then the set of these researches, practices, and experiences, which may be purifications, ascetic exercises, renunciations, conversions of looking, modifications of existence, etc., which are, not for knowledge but for the subject, for the subject's very being, the price to be paid for access to the truth.[20]

This strict correlation between truth and the condition of the Self made it so that the proof of truth could not consist in a merely methodological verification, but would depend also on the characteristics—the mode of being—of the one who pronounced it. Not everyone has access to truth; or better, the access to truth also requires that one is in a particular existential condition. We have seen in chapter 6 how this might be true even for one of the authors most dear to Foucault—Nietzsche. For Foucault, the modality belonging to the practice of truth is that of the parrhesiastes, the one who is capable of speaking the whole truth.[21] Armed with courage, the parrhesiastes—for Foucault the exemplary figure is Socrates—demonstrates the independence of truth from domination, and its constitution as a power of resistance, a countervailing power, capable of limiting its violence.

The ethical virtue of courage thus distinguishes the discourse that is foreign to domination. The process of self-transformation that the parrhesiastes exerts on itself in order to have the right to speak the truth is ultimately a process of liberation from the external power exercised by domination: this is constituted in the very moment when the modality of access to truth is abstracted from concreteness and from the living flow of existence, and becomes a pure, rational criterion. The Cartesian moment, as Foucault calls it, is the moment in which the "purifications" of the Self become amendments of the intellect, in search of a purity of the mind that coincides with its complete transparency, that is, with its self-withdrawal in the face of the "truth in itself." But it is precisely in this way that truth is subjugated to the practices of power and becomes the instrument of domination over real "minds."

In the Gadamerian defense of the extra-methodical character of certain experiences of truth one can safely identify a similar desire to rescue truth from the practices of domination: those formative experiences—in particular art and history—are like this, as they do not at all intend to negate truth, but instead rescue it from its identification with the conditions of methodical rationality, whose characteristics we have seen in chapter 5. Their legitimacy cannot erase the *existential* dimension that the experience of truth entails, and that above all is under scrutiny in the human sciences. The extra-methodical character of these experiences of truth thus plays the same role in Gadamer that the care of self plays in Foucault: that of enacting a transformation. Gadamer tends to describe the transformative power of truth by considering it from the perspective of the object—it is the real itself that transforms—while Foucault considers it from the perspective of the subject, who is transformed by the "rebound effect" that truth enacts upon the one who has the experience. For Gadamer too, no experience of truth really leaves us exactly as we were. And while for Foucault this transformation is still dependent on a *téchne toù bíou,* which is differentiated by instruments of domination due to the fact of being "internal" and not "external" to the subject (but there it could be asked in what sense an ascetic practice is "internal," when it nonetheless entails a rejection and sacrifice of the self), for Gadamer the transformative power of truth is more radically thought as foreign to every methodical practice: it is in fact much more intense than open and upsets every pretense of control over the real. The extra-methodical character is not the negation of truth, but the guarantee of its eccentricity in comparison to domination, or even the condition of its critical power. To say it in other terms: it is the claim on the level of experience of the fact that truth does not coincide with methodical demonstrability, and that it therefore exceeds the ontological domination presupposed by demonstrability—it is more than real.[22]

The term "domination" must therefore be understood here not only in its political significance, but also in its logical one, as a domain, namely, as the preordained realm within which a certain truth is defined, and that therefore limits it and conditions it. This is the sense of what Foucault calls *episteme*: a systemic order made up of determinate practices (methods) and correlative ontological assumptions. Extra-methodical truth points to the possibility of *exceeding* such a realm, of which there are various examples in the history of science: all of those cases in which a certain methodical or ontological domination is placed into crisis by new discoveries and experiences,[23]—in the sense that explicates what is at stake in it once and for all: the irreducibility of something to a given realm—such as the paradigmatic example of the discovery of irrational numbers in ancient Greece. The extra-methodical character is certainly something "irrational"; but this excess is precisely what constitutes the concrete power of liberation and of emancipation that its truth entails.

The extra-methodical character of truth does not however signify its independence from experience. Actually, the more there is truth, the more there is experience. The assertion of the independence of truth from experience (from the access to truth) is often recalled by sustaining that, in the opposite case, it would fall into relativism.[24] But this distinction does not make any sense. Truth is a mode of access to reality (and in this sense it is *alétheia*), but there is not strictly an "access to truth." Truth is a *mode* of experience, not an object, just as the good is a mode of acting. The relation between truth and experience is in fact similar to the relation that, according to Aristotle, exists between the good and ethical action, which constitutes a qualifying point of the Gadamerian conception of truth. The good for Aristotle is not independent of the action that actualizes it, just as it is not independent of the mode of being of the one who performs it. The moment of application is thus constitutive of and not secondary to the very essence of the good. This configuration has made it so that the good, in opposition to what happened in Plato, is in Aristotle greatly exposed to the contingency of existence and thus demonstrates all of its fragility[25]—a condition that lowered ethics to a secondary philosophy, to the point of taking away its status as knowledge.

Truth has not endured a similar fate: it has remained firmly anchored to a metaphysical world of eternal essences, whose foreignness to the world of experience is the guarantee of its logical soundness, that is, of its non-circularity. Every one of its compromises with the world "here below" is seen as irretrievably damaging, a decline into the irrationality of the contingent and the accidental. On the contrary, philosophical hermeneutics has done nothing but bring the ethical schema of the Aristotelian good back into the field of truth. There is no truth without Dasein, and even the mode of "access to truth" is not independent from the praxis of Dasein. If this entails the risk of exposing truth to contingency—the contingency of art and history, both products of human freedom—it can, on the other hand, raise awareness of its fragility: exposed to the abuses of domination and anchored to the mobility of human action. The hermeneutic problematic of truth is placed on this background of radical dynamism, the world marked by movement, by acting, by change, by time: not in order to negate truth, but to negate its metaphysical structure. Thus, confronted with a tone still strongly tragic and in certain ways gigantic, of a clearly stoic stamp, that the relation with truth assumes in the Foucaultian parrhesiastes, in the Gadamerian view truth is rather entrusted, as is the good for Aristotle, to the wisdom of the *phrónimos*: the one who is gifted with that "reasonableness" (*praktische Vernunftigkeit*)[26] capable of dealing with the irrationality of the "here and now," that is, of attending to the *truth of the contingent*.

Notes and Bibliography

Introduction

1. Kant, I. *Critique of Pure Reason*. Translated by Norman Kemp Smith (New York: St. Martin's Press, 1965), 7–8.

2. Ibid., 8.

3. Among more recent publications dealing with this issue one could cite Engel, P., *Truth* (Durham, NC: Acumen, 2002); Marsonet, M., ed., *Il Concetto di verità nel pensiero occidentale* (Genova: Melangolo, 2000); Engel, P., and R. Rorty, *What's the Use of Truth* (New York: Columbia University Press, 2007); D'Agostini, F., *Disavventure della verità* (Torino: Einaudi, 2002); Marconi, D., *Per la verità. Relativismo e filosofia* (Torino: Einaudi, 2007); Vattimo, G., *A Farewell to Truth* (New York: Columbia University Press, 2011).

4. Even Gianni Vattimo, when defining philosophical hermeneutics, uses such an expression: it is a "philosophical theory of the interpretative character of every experience of truth." See Vattimo, G., *Beyond Interpretation* (Stanford, CA: Stanford University Press, 1997), 7.

5. The expression "experience of truth," while rather rare within philosophical literature, is in fact greatly recognized in the literature on intuitionism in the philosophy of mathematics. For example, see Dubucs, J., "Truth and Experience of Truth." In *One Hundred Years of Intuitionism*. Edited by M. van Atten, P. Boldini, M. Bourdeau, and G. Heinzmann (Basil: Birkhäuser, 2008), 49–58.

6. Husserl, E. *Experience and Judgment*. Translated by Spencer Churchill (Evanston, IL: Northwestern University Press, 1973), 19.

7. For Husserl the concepts of "intuition" and "object" are in fact correlative. Cf. Husserl, E. *Ideas Pertaining to a Pure Phenomenology and to a Phenomenological Philosophy* (Dordrecht: Kluwer Academic Publishers, 1998), sec. 3.

8. I deal with this point more specifically in Chiurazzi, G., "L'ipotesi del senso." In *Le ragioni del senso*. Edited by J. Benoist and G. Chiurazzi (Milan/ Udine: Mimesis, 2010), 51–71.

9. Translator's note: Throughout this work the author has translated the German term *Sinn* into the Italian *senso*. The English translation reflects that choice, and thus *Sinn/senso* will be translated as "sense." This is of particular note in the context of Heideggerian thought, as *Sinn* has often been translated into English as "meaning" (most notably, in *die Frage nach dem Sinn von Sein überhaupt*—the question of the meaning of Being).

10. What is in play is, in any case, the simple formal (or, as Kant would say, *nominal*) "definition" of truth, or instead the indication of its necessary conditions (which are always only negative) and also not sufficient (or, instead, positive). On this cf. Parrini, P., "Verità e realtà." In *La verità. Scienza, filosofia, società*. Edited by S. Borutti and L. Fonnesu (Bologna: Il Mulino, 2005), 63–99.

Chapter 1

1. Heidegger, M. *Being and Time*. Translated by John Macquarrie and Edward Robinson (San Francisco: Harper San Francisco, 1962), sec. 6, 44.

2. Ibid., sec. 44, 257.

3. Heidegger, M. *Logic: The Question of Truth*. Translated by T. Sheehan (Bloomington, IN: Indiana University Press, 2010), sec. 15ff.

4. Aristotle. *Categories*, Translated by J. Barnes (Princeton, NJ: Princeton University Press, 1984), 5, 2a11–18.

5. Here I list some of the more important examples: Latin: "Secundae autem substantiae dicuntur, in quibus speciebus illae quae principaliter substantiae dicuntur insunt, hae et harum specierum genera" (*Aristoteles latinus*. Edited by L. Minio-Paluello and translated by Boethius [Bruges-Paris: Desclées de Brouwer, 1961]); "Secunde autem substantie dicuntur species, in quibus speciebus que dicuntur prime substantie existent" (ibid., translated by William of Moerbeke). German: "Zweite Substanzen heißen die Arten, in denen die an erster Stelle Substanzen genannt sind, diese und deren Gattungen" (*Kategorien*. Translated by K. Oehler [Berlin: Akademie Verlag, 1984]). French: "Sont dites essences secondes les espèces auxquelles appartiennent les essences dites au sens premier, ces espèces ainsi que le genre de ces espèces" (*Catégories*. Translated by F. Ildefonse and J. Lallot

[Paris: Seuil, 2002]). Italian: "Invece sono dette sostanze seconde le specie nelle quali esistono quelle che vengon dette sostanze in senso primario; queste ed i generi di questa specie" (*Le Categorie*. Edited by M. Zanatta [Milan: Rizzoli, 1989]). Spanish: "Se llaman substancias segundas las especies a las que pertenecen las llamadas primariamente substancias, tanto esas especies como sus géneros" (*Categorias*. Translated by Luis Ml. Valdés Villanueva [Valencia: Revista Teorema, 1983]). Portuguese: "Por outro lado, chaman-se substâncias segundas as espécies em que estão contidas as substâncias chamadas primeiras, assim como os géneros dessas espécies" (*As Categorias*. Translated by A. Monteiro [Lisboa: 2002]).

6. Aristotle. *Categories* 5, 3a6–7.

7. Ibid., 5, 3a29–32 (modified, substituting "belonging" in the English translation with "existing," as it is in the Italian translation).

8. Cf. Kahn, C. H. "On the Terminology for *Copula* and *Existence*." In *Islamic Philosophy and the Classical Tradition*. Edited by S. M. Stern, A. Hourani, and V. Brown (Columbia, SC: University of South Carolina Press, 1973), 151ff. A similar reconstruction of the meaning of *hypárchein* is undertaken by Tugendhat, E., *TI KATA TINOS. Eine Untersuchung zu Struktur und Ursprung Aristotelischer Grundbegriffe* (Freiburg-München: Alber, 1958), 13n, 14.

9. Ibid., 152.

10. Aristotle. *Categories* 5, 2b6–6c.

11. Aristotle. *Prior Analytics* 1, 24a, 17ff.

12. Aristotle. *Topics* 2, 109a, 10–26.

13. The use of the expression *hypárchei tinì*, Mignucci notes, excludes identity and would in fact be turned to "shed light on the impossibility of interpreting the predicative relation as an identity of subject and predicate." Cf. Aristotle. *Analitici primi*. Translated by M. Mignucci (Naples: Loffredo, 1969), 185, 9n.

14. Melandri, E. *La linea e il circolo. Saggio logico-filosofico sull'analogia* (Macerata: Quodlibet, 2004), 438. This misunderstanding is probably due to the tendency to translate in the same manner, especially in light of the Latin translations of Aristotle, the expressions *hypárchein en tiní* and *hypárchein tiní*.

15. Kahn, C. H. 154. Kahn reports on the case of Sextus Empiricus, who sets up an interesting comparison between *eînai* and *hypárchein* in his discussion of the existence of god: The title of the question, "Do the gods exist?" is written with the verb *eînai*, but immediately after

it is developed by making use of *hypárchein* (*Adv. Math* 9: 29–194ff.). This comparison recalls, including the thematic context, the comparison between *sein* and *dasein* in Kant's essay *The One Possible Argument for Demonstrating the Existence of God*. The verb *hypárchein* thus does not indicate simple being, which would be its specific modality, but real being, the existence of fact, in reality, "in contrast with the simple name or an imaginary object."

16. Boethius. *Commentarii in librum Aristotelis Perì hermeneias*, (Lipsiae: In aedibus B.G. Teubneri, 1880), chap. 3, 67. "[Aristotle] says that the verb is always the sign of that which it predicates of the other, and it is as if to say that verbs could do nothing but signify accidents. In fact every verb signifies an accident. In fact, when I say 'run,' it is a matter of an accident, but it is not said as if it were or were not in someone (*ut id alicui inesse vel non inesse dicatur*). But if I say 'he runs' then I signify as existing in someone (*alicui inesse*) the accident that I place in his action."

17. Leibniz, G. W. "First Truths." In *Shorter Leibniz Texts: A Collection of New Translations* (London, GBR: Continuum International Publishing, 2010), 49. Cf. "Primae veritates." In *Opuscules et fragments inédits*. Edited by L. Couturat (Hildesheim: Olms, 1961), 518.

18. Ibid., 50.

19. Leibniz, G. W. *Discourse on Metaphysics*. Translated by G. Montgomery (La Salle, IL: Open Court Publishing Co., 1990), 13. The same concept is taken up again elsewhere: "And this reason of truth consists in the connection of the predicate with the subject, which is that the predicate is contained in the subject, either manifestly, as in identical propositions, [. . .] or in a hidden manner." Leibniz, G. W. *Opuscules et fragments inédits de Leibniz, extraits des manuscrits de la Bibliothèque royale de Hanovre*. Edited by Louis Couturat (Paris: F. Alcan, 1903), 11.

20. "Quodsi propositio sit contingens, non est necessaria connexio, sed tempore variatur [. . .]" (Ibid., 402).

21. Leibniz, G. W. *Discourse on Metaphysics*. Translated by G. Montgomery (La Salle, IL: Open Court Publishing Co., 1990), 13.

22. Boethius, trans. "De interpretation." *Aristoteles latinus*. Edited by L. Minio-Paluello (Bruges/Paris: Desclée de Brouwer, 1961), vol. 1, 8.

23. Heidegger, M. *Logic: The Question of Truth* (Bloomington, IN: Indiana University Press, 2010), 111.

24. Heidegger, M. *The Fundamental Concepts of Metaphysics: World, Finitude, Solitude.* Translated by W. McNeill and N. Walker (Bloomington, IN: Indiana University Press, 1995), 310.

25. Heidegger, M. *Being and Time*, 271.

26. Ibid., 269.

27. Heidegger, M. *The Fundamental Concepts of Metaphysics*, 340–41.

28. Heidegger, M. *Being and Time*, 271. Donald Davidson expresses a similar idea in the realm of analytic philosophy. Against the mental and the realistic conceptions of truth, he seems to hypothesize an ontological idea similar to the one described by Heidegger, which in fact "carries truth back to earth": "Nothing in the world, no object or event, would be true or false if there were not thinking creatures." Davidson, D. *Truth and Predication* (Cambridge, MA: Harvard University Press, 2005), 7.

29. Heidegger, M. *Being and Time*, 270.

Chapter 2

1. Benveniste, E. *Problems in General Linguistics.* Translated by M. E. Meek (Coral Gables, FL: University of Miami Press, 1971), 143.

2. Ibid., 133 (my italics).

3. Ibid., 133–34.

4. Ibid., 133.

5. Aristotle. *De Interpretatione* 3, 16b24.

6. Ibid., 16b6. The term "verb," as has been noted, translates two Greek words: *lógos* and *rhêma*. In particular, the translation of *lógos* with *verbum* is confirmed by Christianity and above all is valorized by Saint Augustine in reference to the prologue to the Gospel of John (*De diversis quaestionibus*, q. 63), which was contrasted with the North African translations that preferred the use of the term *sermo*. Nevertheless, the Greek correlate of *verbum* is *rhêma* (from *éiro*, "I say," "I speak"), which signifies "word," but also "thing" and "action," and by which technically one indicates the verb as a part of discourse. In an evangelical context, it is rediscovered in Luke 1:37 ("quia non erit impossibile apud Deum omne verbum [*rhêma*]") and 2:15 ("et videamus hoc verbum [*rhêma*], quod factum est, quod Dominus ostendit nobis"). The Greek *rhêma* is a translation of the Hebrew *dāvār*, that, in the same way, signifies "word" and "thing," "event." Philo, however, often renders *dāvār* with *lógos*, and it is here that the connection between *verbum* and *lógos* is probably

affirmed, which pulls the placement of the *verbum-rhêma* relation down to a secondary level.

7. Cf. Sainati, V. *Storia dell'Organon aristotelico*, vol. 1, *Dai* Topici *al* De Interpretatione (Florence: Le Monnier, 1968), 217–18.

8. Aristotle. *De Interpretatione* 5, 17a9–10.

9. Averroes, in his commentary on *De Interpretatione*, observes that in his language, Arabic, the nominal phrase is more frequent than the phrase with a copula, but the copula explicates (*in actu et apparet manifeste*) a joining function that is present (*in potential et subintellectum*) also in the nominal phrase and that carries with it also in the nominal phrase the consignification of a determinate time (Averroes Latinus. *Commentum medium super libro Peri hermeneias Aristotelis*. Edited by R. Hissette [Consejo Superior de Investigaciones Científicas, 1996], 17–18).

10. Cf. Derrida, J. "The Supplement of Copula: Philosophy before Linguistics." In *Margins of Philosophy*. Translated by Alan Bass (Chicago: University of Chicago Press, 1982), where he discusses the essay by Benveniste that was already cited.

11. Chenu, M. D. *La théologie comme science au XIIIe siecle*, 3rd ed. (ParisVrin, 1957), 99–100.

12. Hintikka, J. "Time, Truth, and Knowledge in Aristotle and Other Greek Philosophers." In *Time and Necessity* (Oxford: Clarendon Press, 1973), 64.

13. Aristotle. *De Interpretatione* 3, 16b8–9.

14. Perhaps it is to the aim of "saving" the atemporality of the truths of faith that in medieval Christian philosophy the idea is asserted that the verb always indicates an accident: as Boethius writes, if every verb designates an action or a passion, since the action and the passion are classified among the accidents, "omne [. . .] verbum aliquod accidens designat" (Boethius. *Commentarii in librum Aristotelis Perì hermeneias*, 67). This assertion is discussed by Thomas Aquinas, who observes, however, that according to Aristotle the verb is always the sign of what is predicated of something else—not of what the predicate signifies, but rather of the predication itself, whether it is essential or contingent. Cf. Thomas Aquinas. *In Perì Hermeneias*. Edited by P. Fr. R. M. Spiazzi (Turin: Marietti, 1964), lectio 5, 60.

15. Davidson, D. *Inquiries into Truth and Interpretation*, 2nd ed. (Oxford: Clarendon Press, 2001), 34.

16. De Monticelli, R. "Sulla lingua degli angeli." *Teoria*, 1 (1989), 69–137.

17. Quine, W. v. O. "The Two Dogmas of Empiricism." In *From a Logical Point of View* (New York: Harper and Row, 1963), 40. The problematicity of functional writing, which is not able to eliminate the copula, is also grasped by C. H. Kahn: "It is no accident that *Fa* is commonly read as '*a* is *F*.' And if *this* is what we mean by the verb *be* as a sign of predication, it should be clear that *be* cannot be eliminated from deep structure so long as the deep structure is to retain any analogy with the forms of predicate logic. There must be *something* in the structure of phrases to correspond with the form *Fx*, and hence with *x is F* or *S is P*." Cf. Kahn, C. H. "On the Theory of the Verb 'To be.'" In *Logic and Ontology*. Edited by M. K. Munitz (New York: New York University Press, 1973), 12.

18. Heidegger, M. *History of the Concept of Time*. Translated by T. Kisiel (Bloomington, IN: Indiana University Press, 1985), 57–58.

19. Kant, I. *Critique of Pure Reason*, sec. 19, 159.

20. Ibid., § 19, 158.

21. Ibid., introduction, 41.

22. Picardi, E. "Frege, Peano e Russell sulle idee primitive della logica." In *La filosofia di Gottlob Frege*. Edited by N. Vassallo (Milan: Franco Angeli, 2003), 203. She nonetheless observes that on this point Russell later changes his mind. On this, see Picardi, E. *La chimica dei concetti. Logica, linguaggio, psicologia 1879–1927* (Bologna: Il Mulino, 1994).

23. Ibid., 207.

24. Heidegger, M. *The Fundamental Concepts of Metaphysics*, 325.

25. Hegel, G. W. F. *Phenomenology of Spirit*. Translated by A. V. Miller (Oxford: Oxford University Press, 1977), preface.

26. Hegel, G. W. F. *Faith and Knowledge*. Translated by Walter Cerf (Albany, NY: State University of New York Press, 1977), 72. On Hegel's critique of Kant regarding the Kantian need for a "third term" as the synthetic moment that would have been for him completely formal, cf. Beaufret, J. "Hegel et la proposition speculative." *Dialogue avec Heidegger. Philosophie moderne* (Paris: Les Editions de Minuit, 1973).

27. Hegel, G. W. F. *Phenomenology of Spirit*, 41.

28. Ibid., 42.

29. Ibid.

30. Ibid., 37.

31. Ibid.

32. Ibid., 38.

33. Ibid., 39.

34. Hegel, G. W. F. *Logic: Being Part One of the Encyclopaedia of the Philosophical Sciences*. Translated by W. Wallace (London: Clarendon Press, 1975), sec. 191, 575–77.

35. To what extent the temporality of the speculative proposition represents a "rationalistic" form of temporality (on the model of reversible temporality of rational mechanics), and thus even antithetical to the irreversible one introduced by Christianity, is a question of some importance. On this point allow me to suggest Chiurazzi, G. "Tempo e giustizia. Sulla lettura heideggeriana di Anassimandro." *Etica & Politica/Ethics & Politics* 9, no. 1 (2009), 9–24.

36. Hegel, G. W. F. *Phenomenology of Spirit*, 37.

37. Ibid., 10.

38. Cf. D'Agostini, F. "Pensare con la propria testa. Problemi di filosofia del pensiero in Hegel e Frege." *La filosofia di Gottlob Frege*. Edited by N. Vassallo (Verlag: Franco Angeli, 2003), 59–94.

39. This deals with Brentano's noted theory of double judgment, to which every categorical judgment is divisible in two judgments, one relative to the existence of the object and the other of the predicative type: "Socrates is wise" (∃*x* and F*x*). Such a theory has antecedents in medieval notions, particularly in the doctrine of Thomas Aquinas, who was interpreting the *consignificatio temporis* of the copula as the occurrence of the intentional object to the mind: "In the first place [it] means that which happens in the intellect in the mode of absolute actuality: 'is' signifies 'being in act.'" It is the principle of the intentional in-existence of the object, or even of its imminence to intention, which was also affirmed by Brentano.

40. In section 36 of his lectures on the phenomenology of internal time, Husserl, by capturing the difficulty inherent in attempting to name time, writes that time "is *absolute subjectivity* and has the absolute properties of something to be designated *metaphorically* as 'flow'; [. . .] in the actuality-experience we have the primal source-point and a continuity of moments of reverberation. For all of this, we lack names." Husserl, E. *On the Phenomenology of the Consciousness of Internal Time (1893–1917)*. Translated by J. Brough (Dordrecht: Kluwer Academic Publishers, 1991), 79.

41. Kant, I. *Critique of Pure Reason*, 51.

42. Heidegger, M. *Being and Time*, 269.

43. Ibid., sec. 33, 202.

44. Cf. Chiurazzi, G. "Indecifrabilità e comprensione radicale." *Immagine e scrittura. Filosofia, pittura, schema*. Edited by L. Bagetto and J. C. Lévêque (Rome: Casini Editore, 2009), 99–119.

45. Heidegger, M. *Being and Time*, sec. 32, 193.

Chapter 3

1. "Of course this characterization of truth as 'agreement,' *adequatio, homoíosis*, is very general and empty. Yet it will still have some justification if it can hold its own without prejudice to any of the most various interpretations which that distinctive predicate 'knowledge' will support. We are now inquiring into the foundations of this 'relation.' *What else is tacitly posited in this relational totality of the adequatio intellectus et rei? And what ontological character does that which is thus posited have itself?*" (Heidegger, M. *Being and Time*, 25.)

2. "There can be no affirmation or denial without a verb; for the expressions 'is,' 'will be,' 'was,' 'is coming to be,' and the like are verbs according to our definition, since besides their specific meaning they convey the notion of time." Aristotle. *De Interpretatione* 10, 19b12–14.

3. This elliptical quality of judgment, and in general of every relation to beings, brings about a redefinition of Kant's Copernican Revolution now in terms of a "Keplerian Revolution." Cf. Chiurazzi, G. "Die Keplersche Wende der Hermeneutik." *Alea. Internationale Zeitschrift für Phänomenologie und Hermeneutik* 6, 49–78.

4. Heidegger, M. *Being and Time*, sec. 44, c.

5. "The definition of truth as *adaequatio* is the starting point, not yet the answer; it is the point of departure for posing the problem, but is not yet the solution!" (Heidegger, M. *The Metaphysical Foundations of Logic*. Translated by M. Heim [Bloomington, IN: Indiana University Press, 1984], 125).

6. Heidegger, M. *The Essence of Truth: On Plato's Cave Allegory and Theaetetus*. Translated by T. Sadler (London: Continuum, 2002), 86.

7. Thomas Aquinas. *Summa theologiæ*, I, q.16 (*De veritate*), aa. 1–3.

8. Heidegger, M. *Introduction to Phenomenological Research*. Translated by D. Dahlstrom (Bloomington, IN: Indiana University Press, 2005), 8.

9. Volpi, F. "Editor's Foreword to the Italian Edition." In Heidegger, M. *L'essenza della verità. Sul mito della caverna e sul "Teeteto" di Platone* (Milan: Adelphi, 1997), 16.

10. I believe there are good reasons for connecting the meaning of this alpha privative to the *a* in the word *différance* invented by Derrida: neither, in fact, indicates anything real and literally signify nothing, but mark the fact that something has happened, and they do it by signifying uniquely a difference. For a closer examination of this interpretation of Derridean *différance*, I refer the reader to Chiurazzi, G. "Leggere diversamente. Sinestesia e diagrammaticità della scrittura." *Estetica* 1 (2007), 89–98.

11. Heidegger, M. *The Essence of Truth*, 134.

12. Ibid., 192.

13. Ibid., 162.

14. Ibid.

15. Ibid., 165–66.

16. Heidegger, M. *Contributions to Philosophy (From Enowning)*. Translated by P. Emad and K. Maly (Bloomington, IN: Indiana University Press, 1999), 253ff.

17. Ibid., sec. 228, 249.

18. Heidegger, M. *An Introduction to Metaphysics*. Translated by R. Manheim (New Haven, CT: Yale University Press, 1959). It is clear here that another meaning of metaphysics is introduced—not the metaphysics of the tradition, which is understood as "the science of necessary entities," but one, to a certain degree Kantian, that is an "attitude," a capacity to "go beyond," exactly what in the preceding pages we have seen as the principal capacity of the soul.

19. On this aspect of Heideggerian ontology, I refer the reader to Chiurazzi, G. "La sospensione del reale. *Dynamis* e *symbebekos* nell'ontologia fisica del secondo Heidegger." *Tropos* 2 (2009), 113–29.

20. Heidegger, M. *The Essence of Truth*, 103. This dynamic of *Anwesenheit* and *Abwesenheit* is also at the center of the Heideggerian interpretation of Anaximander. Cf. Heidegger, M. "Anaximander's Saying." *Off the Beaten Track*. Translated by J. Young and K. Hayes (Cambridge: Cambridge University Press, 2002), 242–81.

21. Ibid., 92.

22. Ibid.

23. Ibid., 101–2.

24. It seems this is the way this Heideggerian theory is interpreted in Marconi, D. "On the Mind Dependence of Truth." *Erkenntnis* 65, no. 3 (2006), 301–18.

Chapter 4

1. Cf. Ramsey, F. P. "Facts and Propositions." In *Philosophical Papers*. Edited by D. H. Mellor (Cambridge: Cambridge University Press, 1990); Wittgenstein, L. *Philosophical Investigations*. Translated by G. E. M. Anscombe (Oxford: Blackwell Publishers, 1958), sec. 113.

2. James, W. *Pragmatism* (Amherst, NY: Prometheus Books, 1991), 100.

3. On the possibility of understanding the sign of judgment in these terms, and in fact as a "pure performative operator," cf. Bell, D. *Frege's Theory of Judgment* (Oxford: Blackwell, 1979), 98. Penco, C. *Le vie della scrittura. Frege e la scolta linguistica* (Milan: Franco Angeli, 1994), 66, insists on the fact that the Fregean ideography could be understood as an attempt to formalize the illocutionary *force* connected to speech acts, an idea that was taken up again and developed by Wittgenstein in *Philosophical Investigations* and by the theory of speech acts of Austin and Searle.

4. Frege, G. "Thoughts." In *Logical Investigations*. Translated by P. T. Geach and R. H. Stoothoff (New Haven, CT: Yale University Press, 1977), 6.

5. Vattimo, G. *Il soggetto e la maschera. Nietzsche e il problema della liberazione* (Milan: Bompiani, 1984), chap. 3.

6. Cf. James, W. *Pragmatism*, xx.

7. Rorty, R. *Consequences of Pragmatism* (Minneapolis, MN: University of Minnesota Press, 1982), 5.

8. Cf. Ibid., "Introduction: Pragmatism and Philosophy," 31n, xlvi. On the theme of the uselessness of the word "Being" and of the copula in Berkeley, I direct the reader to Chiurazzi, G. "L'essere inutile. Il problema della mediazione in George Berkeley." *Filosofia* 1 (1998), 53–75.

9. Rorty, R. "Mind-Body Identity, Privacy and Categories." *The Review of Metaphysics* 19 (1965); "In Defense of Eliminative Materialism." *The Review of Metaphysics*, 24 (1970); both republished in *Materialism and the Mind-Body Problem*. Edited by David M. Rosenthal (Englewood Cliffs, NJ: Prentice Hall, 1971).

10. "The wheel that turns idly" is characterized by a relation of "indifference" with respect to "positive" experience; or because it is a linguistic element lacking *real* representative function, that is, a function non-essential for representation or not referred to *actual* representation, or because it is an assertion that cannot be confirmed or denied in experience. Cf. Marconi, G. *Wittgenstein e le ruote che girano a vuoto*, in *Il pensiero debole*. Edited by G. Vattimo and P. A. Rovatti (Milan: Feltrinelli, 1983), 169.

11. Rorty, R. *Consequences of Pragmatism*, 23.

12. James, W. *Pragmatism*, 138.

13. Rorty, R. *Consequences of Pragmatism*, 17. Cf. also W. James, where he writes that according to pragmatic ends there is no difference between "it is true because it works and it works because it is true." James, W. *Pragmatism*, 140.

14. Ibid., 17.

15. Vattimo's distinction between "truth as opening" and "the opening as truth," which he discusses in "The Truth of Hermeneutics" (in *Beyond Interpretation*, 77ff), seems to a great extent applicable to these conceptual copies. In fact, I would say that it is nothing but the explanation of the difference between *the true experience* (which is such by virtue of a constant opening to truth) and *true experience* (which is a determinate, meaningful dimension within experience).

16. On this possibility of understanding hermeneutics as the consequence of critical rationalism, see the debate between Albert, H. and J. Grondin in *Hermeneutik und Naturalismus*. Edited by B. Kanitscheider and F. J. Wetz, in collaboration with B. Suchan (Tübingen: Mohr, 1998).

17. Heidegger, M. *Phenomenology of Religious Life*. Translated by M. Fritsch and J. A. Gosetti-Ferencei (Bloomington, IN: Indiana University Press, 2010), 85.

18. Gadamer, H. G. "Introduzione." *Verità e metodo*, 3rd ed. Translated by G. Vattimo (Milan: Bompiani, 1986), viii.

19. Translator's note: In Italian, the meaning of "true" is doubled in two different syntactical placements of the word, either before or after the word "experience." One could also consider the distinction as one between "true experience" (*esperienza vera*) and "real experience" (*vera esperienza*).

20. Cf. James, W. *Pragmatism*, 154–56.

21. Rorty, R. *Consequences of Pragmatism*, 5.

22. Heidegger, M. "Plato's Doctrine of Truth." In *Pathmarks*. Edited by W. McNeill (Cambridge: Cambridge University Press, 1998), 166.

23. Ibid., 165.

24. Ibid.

25. "An interpretation decisive for Western thought is that given by Plato. He says that between beings and Being there prevails the *chorismós*; *he chóra* is the locus, the site, the place. Plato means to say: beings and Being are differently located. Thus when Plato gives thought to the different location of beings and Being, he is asking for the totally different place of Being, as against

the place of beings." Heidegger, M. *What Is Called Thinking?* Translated by J. Glenn Gray (New York: Harper and Row Publishers, 1968), 227.

26. Heidegger, M. "Plato's Doctrine of Truth," 167–68.

27. Rorty, R. *Philosophy and the Mirror of Nature* (Princeton, NJ: Princeton University Press, 1979), 360ff.

28. Cf. Rorty, R. "Analytic and Conversational Philosophy." *Philosophy as Cultural Politics* (Cambridge: Cambridge University Press, 2007), 120–30.

29. Cf. Eco, U. *Interpretation and Overinterpretation* (Cambridge: Cambridge University Press, 1992), 145.

30. Rorty, R. *Consequences of Pragmatism*, xiv, xxxi.

31. On the role that the notion of truth plays in Gadamer, to the point of it being at the greatest distance from Rorty's views, see Prado, C. G. "Gadamer and Rorty: From Interpretation to Conversation." In *Consequences of Hermeneutics: Fifty Years after Gadamer's* Truth and Method. Edited by J. Malpas and S. Zabala (Evanston, IL: Northwestern University Press, 2010), 147–60.

32. Vattimo, G., and P. Paterlini. *Not Being God: A Collaborative Autobiography* (New York: Columbia University Press, 2009), 135.

Chapter 5

1. Gadamer, H. G. *Reason in the Age of Science*. Translated by F. G. Lawrence (Cambridge, MA: MIT Press, 1983), 70.

2. Kant, I. *Critique of Pure Reason*, xiii.

3. Apel, K. O., et al. "Szientifik, Hermeneutik, Ideologie-Kritik: Entwurf einer Wissenschaftslehre in erkenntnisanthropologischer Sicht." *Hermeneutik und Ideologiekritik* (Frankfurt am Main: Suhrkamp Verlag, 1971), 9.

4. On the various articulations of truth as openness in Heidegger, cf. Heefer, P. "Heidegger's Discussion with Husserl on the Being of Truth in §44 of *Sein und Zeit*." *Heidegger and Husserl in Vergleich*. Edited by F. Rese (Frankfurt a.M.: Klostermann, 2010), 198.

5. In this way, Heidegger describes experience in its most minimal form, what is farthest from the conception of experience as "experiment": "'experiencing': striking up against something and indeed something that strikes us; having to take in something that comes upon us and does something to us, 'affects' us, encounters us without our complicity." Heidegger, M. *Contributions to Philosophy (Of the Event)*. Translated by R. Rojcewicz and D. Vallega-Neu (Bloomington, IN: Indiana University Press, 2010), sec. 77.

6. On this distinction, cf. Eco, U. "Huizinga e il gioco." *Homo ludens* (Turin: Einaudi, 1973). The fact that Wittgenstein prefers to speak of *game* (*language games*) therefore constitutes an important symptom for understanding its difference from Gadamer's notion of play: the game for Wittgenstein is in fact understood first of all as a set of rules, while for Gadamer it is the game as it is played out.

7. Gadamer, H. G. *Truth and Method.* Translated by Joel Weinsheimer and Donald G. Marshall (London and New York: Continuum, 2006), 123.

8. Ibid., 85.

9. Ibid., 89.

10. It is interesting to note how this correlation between experimental technics and aesthetic consciousness is also foreseen by Heidegger in the form of a correlation between machination (*Machenschaft*) and lived experience (*Erlebnis*) in *Contributions to Philosophy*: here Heidegger singles out the connection in the idea according to which only that which is subjected to machination is really an entity, that is, only what is subjected to the mastery of man, placed "in front" of him, re-presented in the sense of *Vorstellung* (Heidegger, M. *Contributions to Philosophy*, sec. 61ff.).

11. Re-presentation (when written with the hyphen) is intended here not in the sense of *Vorstellung*, but again in the sense of *Darstellung*: the work of art needs to be "re-presented," exhibited, again and again, as in the case of a theatrical presentation or a game. This sort of "re-actualization" of the work of art is the core of Gadamer's aesthetic ontology, which conceives of the work of art, not in its reference to an original, and then as representation (*Vorstellung*), but as event, which with its presentation adds, as we will see, something more to the original.

12. Gadamer, H. G. *Truth and Method*, 123.

13. Ibid., 137.

14. Ibid.

15. It is for this reason that Eco rejects the idea that reflected images can be understood as signs, and for that reason as semiotic objects. Cf. Eco, U. *Sugli specchi e altri saggi* (Milan: Bompiani, 1985).

16. Gadamer, H. G. *Truth and Method*, 140.

17. Cf. Rorty, R. *Philosophy and the Mirror of Nature.*

18. Here arises the idea, for Gadamer, that the subject cannot be understood as a simple mirror, due to its finitude and situatedness. If worse comes to worst, it can be conceived as a "distorting mirror": "Long before we understand ourselves through the process of self-examination, we understand ourselves

in a self-evident way in the family, society, and state in which we live. The focus of subjectivity is a distorting mirror. The self-awareness of the individual is only a flickering in the closed circuits of historical life" (Gadamer, H. G. *Truth and Method*, 276).

19. Ibid., 135 (translation modified).

20. Ibid.

21. Ibid.

22. Ibid., 114.

23. Ibid.

24. Ibid., 12.

25. Ibid., 113.

26. Ibid., 356. On this point, in a note in the second edition of *Truth and Method*, Gadamer makes explicit reference to Karl Popper's paired concepts of *trial and error*, "with the restriction that those concepts all too often proceed from the deliberate, and all too rarely from the suffering side of human experience of life" (115n, 380). The parallelism between the Gadamerian concept of experience and Popperian falsificationism has been shown by Grondin, J. "Die Hermeneutik als die Konsequenz des kritischen Rationalismus." *Hermeneutik und Naturalismus*. Edited by B. Kanitscheider and F. J. Wetz (Tübingen: Mohr, 1998).

27. I prefer to translate the Gadamerian expression "*Verwandlung ins Gebilde*" with "transmutation into form," and not with "transformation into structure" (as the English translation does). The word "structure" has mechanical nuances that risk laying aside the vitalistic and organicistic meaning of the word "form," which is surely present in the general idea of an "increase into being" as a consequence of a "transmutation."

28. Gadamer, H. G. *Truth and Method*, 111 (modified).

29. Ibid., 114.

30. Ibid., 112 (modified).

31. "Through Newton the laws became true and with them, entities became accessible in themselves to Dasein. Once entities have been uncovered, they show themselves precisely as entities which beforehand already were" (Heidegger, M. *Being and Time*, 269).

32. Davidson, D. *Truth and Predication* (Cambridge, MA: Harvard University Press, 2005), 27.

33. It is also interesting to note that Davidson, in vindicating the nonredundant nature of "true," even in the Tarskian theory, has recourse just to a pictorial metaphor: saying "true" is like adding "another brush-stroke to the

picture [. . .]. What appears to the right of the biconditional in sentences of the form 's is true if and only if p' when such sentences are consequences of a theory of truth plays its role in determining the meaning of s not by pretending synonymy but by adding one more brush-stroke to the picture which, taken as a whole, tells what there is to know of the meaning of s; this stroke is added by virtue of the fact that the sentence that replaces 'p' is true if and only if s is." (Davidson, D. *Inquiries into Truth and Interpretation* [Oxford: Clarendon Press, 1984], 26).

34. At most, as Kant observes, its necessary, namely negative, conditions can be identified, but not the sufficient, namely positive, ones (cf. Kant, I. *Critique of Pure Reason*, 97–98).

35. This idea implicates a relation between mode, operator, and disposition that I addressed in Chiurazzi, G. *Modalità e esistenza. Dalla critica della ragion pura alla critica della ragione ermeneutica* (Rome: Aracne, 2009), especially in chapter 1.

36. Gadamer, H. G. *Truth and Method*, 12.

37. Ibid.

38. Ibid., 355.

39. Ibid., 362.

Chapter 6

1. On this performative dimension of language, see Benoist, J. "Senso e *performance*." *Le ragioni del senso*. Edited by J. Benoist and G. Chiurazzi (Milan-Udine: Mimesis, 2010), 159–74.

2. Deleuze, G. *Nietzsche and Philosophy*. Translated by H. Tomlinson (New York: Columbia University Press, 2006), 3.

3. Ibid., 4.

4. Cf. Vattimo, G. *Nietzsche: An Introduction*. Translated by N. Martin (Stanford, CA: Stanford University Press, 2001), 9–11.

5. Nietzsche, F. *Beyond Good and Evil: Prelude to a Philosophy of the Future* (Cambridge, MA: Cambridge University Press, 2002), sec. 211, 105

6. Deleuze, G. *Nietzsche and Philosophy*, 2.

7. Kant, I. *Critique of Pure Reason*, 314. I owe Robert Valgenti for having turned my attention to this point of Kantian critique during a seminar held on June 14, 2007, in Turin entitled "La deduzione ermeneutica." now published in *Tropos* 1 (*Dialogo e conflitto*, edited by G. Chiurazzi, 2009), 127–39.

8. Vattimo, G. *Nietzsche: An Introduction*, 79.

9. Nietzsche, F. *Human, All Too Human*. Translated by R. J. Hollingdale (Cambridge, MA: Cambridge University Press, 1996), sec. 20, 23.

10. Ibid., sec. 34, 30.

11. Vattimo, G. *Nietzsche: An Introduction,* 83.

12. Nietzsche, F. *Daybreak: Thoughts on the Prejudices of Morality*. Translated by R. J. Hollingdale (Cambridge, MA: Cambridge University Press, 1997), sec. 42, 30; sec. 102, 59.

13. Ibid., sec. 424, 181.

14. Ibid., sec. 424, 181–82.

15. Ibid.

16. Ibid., sec. 322, 323.

17. Ibid., 151.

18. Nietzsche, F. "On Truth and Lies in a Nonmoral Sense." *The Birth of Tragedy and Other Writings*. Edited by R. Guess and R. Speirs (Cambridge, MA: Cambridge University Press, 1999), 146.

19. Nietzsche, F. *Daybreak*, sec. 103, 60.

20. Giorgio, C., et al. *Werke. Kritische Gesamtausgabe. Band 1 Nachgelassene Fragmente Juli 1882—Winter 1883—1884* (Berlin: De Gruyter, 1977), 16 (60).

21. For further development of this interpretation of the eternal return, which reads it as a selective experiment of a new form of humanity, I refer the reader to Chiurazzi, G. "The Experiment of Nihilism: Interpretation and Experience of Truth in Gianni Vattimo." In *Between Nihilism and Politics: The Hermeneutics of Gianni Vattimo*. Edited by S. Benso and B. Schroeder (Albany: SUNY Press, 2010), 15–32.

22. Nietzsche, F. *Human, All Too Human*, sec. 34, 30.

23. Nietzsche, F. "On Truth and Lies in a Nonmoral Sense," 145.

24. Deleuze, G. *Nietzsche and Philosophy*, 89.

Chapter 7

1. Cf. Putnam, H. *Reason, Truth, and History* (Cambridge, MA: Cambridge University Press, 1981), 49.

2. Ibid., xi.

3. Ibid., 50.

4. The idea that the predicate of truth is a monadic predicate, and that it therefore applies *simpliciter* to propositions, understood as objects of

propositional attitudes, is defended particularly in the book of Cappelen, H. and J. Hawthorne. *Relativism and Monadic Truth* (Oxford: Oxford University Press, 2009).

5. Putnam shows the unsustainability of metaphysical realism through his thought experiment of brains in a vat: a metaphysical realist could not respond to the question "*from whose point of view is the story being told?*" and so simply avoids it (cf. Putnam, H. *Reason, Truth, and History*, 50).

6. Gadamer, H. G. *Truth and Method*, 108.

7. Ibid., 108.

8. This distinction between a subjective "for me" and an objective "for me" (I think) is analogous to the distinction that Kant traces between judgments of perception and judgments of experience (cf. Kant, I. *Prolegomena to Any Future Metaphysics*, rev. ed. Edited by G. Hatfield (Cambridge, MA: Cambridge University Press, 2004), sec. 18ff. On the transcendental significance of "for," cf. sec. 2.3.

9. Cf. Chiurazzi, G. *Modalità ed esistenza*, chapter 5. The sense of this *convenientia* could also be expressed in terms of what Saul Kripke called "a priori contingency" or "a posteriori necessity": a correlation that is a priori completely contingent but that is recognized as the necessary condition of what follows from it.

10. Thomas Aquinas. *Summa theological* 1, q. 16 (*De veritate*), 1–3.

11. Putnam, H. *Reason, Truth, and History*, 49.

12. It is as D. Davidson also observes, affirming the need for integration with the Tarskian theory of truth, so that speakers are also taken into consideration, without whom there would no longer be any truth: "What is missing is the connection with the users of language. Nothing would count as a sentence, and the concept of truth would have no application, if there were not creatures who used sentences by uttering or inscribing tokens of them." Davidson, D. *Truth and Predication* (Cambridge, MA: Harvard University Press, 2005), 36.

13. Husserl, E. *Logical Investigations*. Translated by N. Findlay (New York: Routledge, 2001), vol. 1, sec. 39, 86.

14. On this, see Baldwin, T. "Three Puzzles in Frege's Theory of Truth." *Frege: Sense and Reference One Hundred Years Later*. Edited by J. Biro and P. Kotatko (Berlin: Kluwer, 1995), 1–14.

15. Gros, F. "Verità, soggettività, filosofia nell'ultimo Foucault." *Foucault oggi*. Edited by M. Galzigna (Milan: Feltrinelli, 2008), 301.

16. Cf. Foucault, M. *Discipline and Punish: The Birth of the Prison*. Translated by A. Sheridan (New York: Random House, 1977); *The History of Sexuality. Volume 1: An Introduction*. Translated by R. Hurley (New York: Random House), 1978.

17. Engel, P, and R. Roty. *What's the Use of Truth*, 24–25.

18. Cf. in particular Foucault, M. *The History of Sexuality, Volume 3: The Care of the Self* (New York: Pantheon Books, 1986); *The Hermeneutics of the Subject: Lectures at the Collège de France 1981–1982* (London: Picador, 2005); *The Courage of Truth: The Government of Self and Others II; Lectures at the Collège de France, 1983–1984* (London: Picador, 2012).

19. Foucault singles out in Plato the moment in which the process of the philosophical resolution of truth begins: the limit of his reconstruction is nevertheless precisely in the fact that in Plato the experience of truth, as we have underlined several times when speaking about the myth of the cave, is not a process of training but a process of liberation, which entails a radical transformation of the human, that radical existential modification that Foucault attributes not to philosophy, but to spirituality.

20. Foucault, M. *The Hermeneutics of the Subject*, 15.

21. Foucault, M. *Discourse and Truth: The Problematization of Parrhesia*. Edited by J. Pearson (Los Angeles, CA: Semiotext(e), 2001).

22. As is noted, this deals with the translation of one of the results of Gödel's theorems onto the experiential level.

23. Exactly in these terms, and that is as a process of revision of one's own ontological and methodological presuppositions, Heidegger describes the progress of the sciences in section 3 of *Being and Time*: "The real 'movement' of the sciences takes place when their basic concepts undergo a more or less radical revision which is transparent to itself. The level which a science has reached is determined by how far it is *capable* of a crisis in its basic concepts. In such immanent crises the very relationship between positively investigative inquiry (that is, the method) and those things themselves that are under interrogation (the presupposed ontology) comes to a point where it begins to totter." Heidegger, M. *Being and Time*, sec. 3, 29. I have added the content in parentheses.

24. Cf. Marconi, D. *Per la verità*, 64ff. Marconi argues that to assert the dependence of truth on the mind means violating Tarski's principle, according to which "*p* is true if and only if *p*." But the question is that if there were no mind, there would also be no Tarskian principle (what would *p* mean in a world without minds?), which therefore would not be able to be violated

at all. Tarski's principle presupposes precisely that there is a mind, as with every theory that relies "purely" on correspondence. My impression is that in Marconi's argument reality and truth are identified according to that principle of equivalence that I have tried to challenge here: truth is more than the real precisely because it is about the real made accessible for someone. But "for" someone is not the truth: if anything it is truth that supposes that the real is "for" someone. At least one.

25. Nussbaum, M. *The Fragility of Goodness: Luck and Ethics in Greek Tragedy and Philosophy* (Cambridge, MA: Cambridge University Press, 1986).

26. Cf. Aristoteles. *Nikomachische Ethik VI*. German translation by H. G. Gadamer (Frankfurt a.M.: Klostermann, 1998). On the relation between *phrónesis* and contingency, cf. Aubenque, P. *La prudence chez Aristote* (Paris: P.U.F., 2002), chapter 3.

Index